A Prentice Hall Pocket Reader

THEMES

Edited by

Clyde Moneyhun

University of Delaware

PEARSON

Prentice
Hall

Upper Saddle River, New Jersey 07458

© 2005 by PEARSON EDUCATION, INC.
Upper Saddle River, New Jersey 07458

ISBN 0-13-240005-7

Printed in the United States of America

CONTENTS

1

PEOPLE

MY FATHER'S LIFE

Raymond Carver

My dad's name was Clevie Raymond Carver. His family called 1
him Raymond and friends called him C. R. I was named Raymond
Clevie Carver Jr. I hated the "Junior" part. When I was little my dad
called me Frog, which was okay. But later, like everybody else in the
family, he began calling me Junior. He went on calling me this until I
was thirteen or fourteen and announced that I wouldn't answer to
that name any longer. So he began calling me Doc. From then until
his death, on June 17, 1967, he called me Doc, or else Son.

When he died, my mother telephoned my wife with the news. I 2
was away from my family at the time, between lives, trying to enroll
in the School of Library Science at the University of Iowa. When my
wife answered the phone, my mother blurted out. "Raymond's
dead!" For a moment, my wife thought my mother was telling her
that I was dead. Then my mother made it clear *which* Raymond she
was talking about and my wife said, "Thank God. I thought you
meant *my* Raymond."

My dad walked, hitched rides, and rode in empty boxcars when 3
he went from Arkansas to Washington State in 1934, looking for
work. I don't know whether he was pursuing a dream when he went
out to Washington. I doubt it. I don't think he dreamed much. I
believe he was simply looking for steady work at decent pay. Steady
work was meaningful work. He picked apples for a time and then
landed a construction laborer's job on the Grand Coulee Dam.[1] After
he'd put aside a little money, he bought a car and drove back to

---

[1] On the Columbia River, northwest of Spokane, Washington.

Arkansas to help his folks, my grandparents, pack up for the move west. He said later that they were about to starve down there, and this wasn't meant as a figure of speech. It was during that short while in Arkansas, in a town called Leola, that my mother met my dad on the sidewalk as he came out of a tavern.

"He was drunk," she said. "I don't know why I let him talk to me. His eyes were glittery. I wish I'd had a crystal ball." They'd met once, a year or so before, at a dance. He'd had girlfriends before her, my mother told me. "Your dad always had a girlfriend, even after we married. He was my first and last. I never had another man. But I didn't miss anything." 4

They were married by a justice of the peace on the day they left for Washington, this big, tall country girl and a farmhand-turned-construction worker. My mother spent her wedding night with my dad and his folks, all of them camped beside the road in Arkansas. 5

In Omak, Washington, my dad and mother lived in a little place not much bigger than a cabin. My grandparents lived next door. My dad was still working on the dam, and later, with the huge turbines producing electricity and the water backed up for a hundred miles into Canada, he stood in the crowd and heard Franklin D. Roosevelt when he spoke at the construction site. "He never mentioned those guys who died building that dam," my dad said. Some of his friends had died there, men from Arkansas, Oklahoma, and Missouri. 6

He then took a job in a sawmill in Clatskanie, Oregon, a little town alongside the Columbia River. I was born there, and my mother has a picture of my dad standing in front of the gate to the mill, proudly holding me up to face the camera. My bonnet is on crooked and about to come untied. His hat is pushed back on his forehead, and he's wearing a big grin. Was he going in to work or just finishing his shift? It doesn't matter. In either case, he had a job and a family. These were his salad days. 7

In 1941 we moved to Yakima, Washington, where my dad went to work as a saw filer, a skilled trade he'd learned in Clatskanie. When war broke out, he was given a deferment because his work was considered necessary to the war effort. Finished lumber was in demand by the armed services, and he kept his saws so sharp they could shave the hair off your arm. 8

After my dad had moved us to Yakima, he moved his folks into the same neighborhood. By the mid-1940s the rest of my dad's family—his brother, his sister, and her husband, as well as uncles, cousins, nephews, and most of their extended family and friends— 9 had come out from Arkansas. All because my dad came out first. The men went to work at Boise Cascade, where my dad worked, and the women packed apples in the canneries. And in just a little while, it seemed—according to my mother—everybody was better off than my dad. "Your dad couldn't keep money," my mother said. "Money burned a hole in his pocket. He was always doing for others."

The first house I clearly remember living in, at 1515 South 10 Fifteenth Street, in Yakima, had an outdoor toilet. On Halloween night, or just any night, for the hell of it, neighbor kids, kids in their early teens, would carry our toilet away and leave it next to the road. My dad would have to get somebody to help him bring it home. Or these kids would take the toilet and stand it in somebody else's backyard. Once they actually set it on fire. But ours wasn't the only house that had an outdoor toilet. When I was old enough to know what I was doing, I threw rocks at the other toilets when I'd see someone go inside. This was called bombing the toilets. After a while, though, everyone went to indoor plumbing until, suddenly, our toilet was the last outdoor one in the neighborhood. I remember the shame I felt when my third-grade teacher, Mr. Wise, drove me home from school one day. I asked him to stop at the house just before ours, claiming I lived there.

I can recall what happened one night when my dad came home 11 late to find that my mother had locked all the doors on him from the inside. He was drunk, and we could feel the house shudder as he rattled the door. When he'd managed to force open a window, she hit him between the eyes with a colander and knocked him out. We could see him down there on the grass. For years afterward, I used to pick up this colander—it was as heavy as a rolling pin—and imagine what it would feel like to be hit in the head with something like that.

It was during this period that I remember my dad taking me into 12 the bedroom, sitting me down on the bed, and telling me that I might have to go live with my Aunt La Von for a while. I couldn't understand what I'd done that meant I'd have to go away from home to live. But this, too—whatever prompted it—must have blown over, more or less, anyway, because we stayed together, and I didn't have to go live with her or anyone else.

I remember my mother pouring his whiskey down the sink. 13 Sometimes she'd pour it all out and sometimes, if she was afraid of getting caught, she'd only pour half of it out and then add water to the rest. I tasted some of his whiskey once myself. It was terrible stuff, and I don't see how anybody could drink it.

After a long time without one, we finally got a car, in 1949 or 14
1950, a 1938 Ford. But it threw a rod the first week we had it, and my
dad had to have the motor rebuilt.

"We drove the oldest car in town," my mother said. "We could 15
have had a Cadillac for all he spent on car repairs." One time she
found someone else's tube of lipstick on the floorboard, along with a
lacy handkerchief. "See this?" she said to me. "Some floozy left this
in the car."

Once I saw her take a pan of warm water into the bedroom 16
where my dad was sleeping. She took his hand from under the covers and held it in the water. I stood in the doorway and watched. I
wanted to know what was going on. This would make him talk in his
sleep, she told me. There were things she needed to know, things she
was sure he was keeping from her.

Every year or so, when I was little, we would take the North 17
Coast Limited across the Cascade Range from Yakima to Seattle and
stay in the Vance Hotel and eat, I remember, at a place called the
Dinner Bell Cafe. Once we went to Ivar's Acres of Clams and drank
glasses of warm clam broth.

In 1956, the year I was to graduate from high school, my dad quit 18
his job at the mill in Yakima and took a job in Chester, a little sawmill
town in northern California. The reasons given at the time for his taking the job had to do with a higher hourly wage and the vague
promise that he might, in a few years' time, succeed to the job of head
filer in this new mill. But I think, in the main, that my dad had grown
restless and simply wanted to try his luck elsewhere. Things had got-
ten a little too predictable for him in Yakima. Also, the year before,
there had been the deaths, within six months of each other, of both
his parents.

But just a few days after graduation, when my mother and I were 19
packed to move to Chester, my dad penciled a letter to say he'd been
sick for a while. He didn't want us to worry, he said, but he'd cut
himself on a saw. Maybe he'd got a tiny sliver of steel in his blood.
Anyway, something had happened and he'd had to miss work, he
said. In the same mail was an unsigned postcard from somebody
down there telling my mother that my dad was about to die and that
he was drinking "raw whiskey."

When we arrived in Chester, my dad was living in a trailer that 20
belonged to the company. I didn't recognize him immediately. I guess
for a moment I didn't want to recognize him. He was skinny and pale
and looked bewildered. His pants wouldn't stay up. He didn't look

like my dad. My mother began to cry. My dad put his arm around her and patted her shoulder vaguely, like he didn't know what this was all about, either. The three of us took up life together in the trailer, and we looked after him as best we could. But my dad was sick, and he couldn't get any better. I worked with him in the mill that summer and part of the fall. We'd get up in the mornings and eat eggs and toast while we listened to the radio, and then go out the door with our lunch pails. We'd pass through the gate together at eight in the morning, and I wouldn't see him again until quitting time. In November I went back to Yakima to be closer to my girlfriend, the girl I'd made up my mind I was going to marry.

He worked at the mill in Chester until the following February, 21 when he collapsed on the job and was taken to the hospital. My mother asked if I would come down there and help. I caught a bus from Yakima to Chester, intending to drive them back to Yakima. But now, in addition to being physically sick, my dad was in the midst of a nervous breakdown, though none of us knew to call it that at the time. During the entire trip back to Yakima, he didn't speak, not even when asked a direct question. ("How do you feel, Raymond?" "You okay, Dad?") He'd communicate if he communicated at all, by moving his head or by turning his palms up as if to say he didn't know or care. The only time he said anything on the trip, and for nearly a month afterward, was when I was speeding down a gravel road in Oregon and the car muffler came loose. "You were going too fast," he said.

Back in Yakima a doctor saw to it that my dad went to a psychi- 22 atrist. My mother and dad had to go on relief,[2] as it was called, and the county paid for the psychiatrist. The psychiatrist asked my dad. "Who is the President?" He'd had a question put to him that he could answer. "Ike," my dad said. Nevertheless, they put him on the fifth floor of Valley Memorial Hospital and began giving him electroshock treatments. I was married by then and about to start my own family. My dad was still locked up when my wife went into this same hospital, just one floor down, to have our first baby. After she had delivered, I went upstairs to give my dad the news. They let me in through a steel door and showed me where I could find him. He was sitting on a couch with a blanket over his lap. *Hey*, I thought. *What in hell is happening to my dad?* I sat down next to him and told him he was a grandfather. He waited a minute and then he said, "I feel like a

---

[2] What would today be called "public assistance" or "welfare."

grandfather." That's all he said. He didn't smile or move. He was in a big room with a lot of other people. Then I hugged him, and he began to cry.

Somehow he got out of there. But now came the years when he couldn't work and just sat around the house trying to figure what next and what he'd done wrong in his life that he'd wound up like this. My mother went from job to crummy job. Much later she referred to that time he was in the hospital, and those years just afterward, as "when Raymond was sick." The word *sick* was never the same for me again.

In 1964, through the help of a friend, he was lucky enough to be hired on at a mill in Klamath, California. He moved down there by himself to see if he could hack it. He lived not far from the mill, in a one-room cabin not much different from the place he and my mother had started out living in when they went west. He scrawled letters to my mother, and if I called she'd read them aloud to me over the phone. In the letters, he said it was touch and go. Every day that he went to work, he felt like it was the most important day of his life. But every day, he told her, made the next day that much easier. He said for her to tell me he said hello. If he couldn't sleep at night, he said, he thought about me and the good times we used to have. Finally, after a couple of months, he regained some of his confidence. He could do the work and didn't think he had to worry that he'd let anybody down ever again. When he was sure, he sent for my mother.

He'd been off from work for six years and had lost everything in that time—home, car, furniture, and appliances, including the big freezer that had been my mother's pride and joy. He'd lost his good name too—Raymond Carver was someone who couldn't pay his bills—and his self-respect was gone. He'd even lost his virility. My mother told my wife, "All during that time Raymond was sick we slept together in the same bed, but we didn't have relations. He wanted to a few times, but nothing happened. I didn't miss it, but I think he wanted to, you know."

During those years I was trying to raise my own family and earn a living. But, one thing and another, we found ourselves having to move a lot. I couldn't keep track of what was going down in my dad's life. But I did have a chance one Christmas to tell him I wanted to be a writer. I might as well have told him I wanted to become a plastic surgeon. "What are you going to write about?" he wanted to know. Then, as if to help me out, he said, "Write about stuff you know about. Write about some of those fishing trips we took." I said I would, but I knew I wouldn't. "Send me what you write," he said. I said I'd do that, but then I didn't. I wasn't writing anything about fishing, and I didn't think he'd particularly care about, or even necessarily understand, what I was writing in those days. Besides, he wasn't a reader. Not the sort, anyway, I imagined I was writing for.

Then he died. I was a long way off, in Iowa City, with things still 27 to say to him. I didn't have the chance to tell him goodbye, or that I thought he was doing great at his new job. That I was proud of him for making a comeback.

My mother said he came in from work that night and ate a big 28 supper. Then he sat at the table by himself and finished what was left of a bottle of whiskey, a bottle she found hidden in the bottom of the garbage under some coffee grounds a day or so later. Then he got up and went to bed, where my mother joined him a little later. But in the night she had to get up and make a bed for herself on the couch. "He was snoring so loud I couldn't sleep," she said. The next morning when she looked in on him, he was on his back with his mouth open, his cheeks caved in. *Graylooking,* she said. She knew he was dead—she didn't need a doctor to tell her that. But she called one anyway, and then she called my wife.

Among the pictures my mother kept of my dad and herself dur- 29 ing those early days in Washington was a photograph of him standing in front of a car, holding a beer and a stringer of fish. In the photograph he is wearing his hat back on his forehead and has this awkward grin on his face. I asked her for it and she gave it to me, along with some others. I put it up on my wall, and each time we moved, I took the picture along and put it up on another wall. I looked at it carefully from time to time, trying to figure out some things about my dad, and maybe myself in the process. But I couldn't. My dad just kept moving further and further away from me and back into time. Finally, in the course of another move, I lost the photograph. It was then that I tried to recall it, and at the same time make an attempt to say something about my dad, and how I thought that in some important ways we might be alike. I wrote the poem when I was living in an apartment house in an urban area south of San Francisco, at a time when I found myself, like my dad, having trouble with alcohol. The poem was a way of trying to connect up with him.

Photograph of My Father in His Twenty-Second Year

October. Here in this dank, unfamiliar kitchen
I study my father's embarrassed young man's face.
Sheepish grin, he holds in one hand a string
of spiny yellow perch, in the other
a bottle of Carlsberg beer.   5

In jeans and flannel shirt, he leans
against the front fender of a 1934 Ford.
He would like to pose brave and hearty for his posterity,
wear his old hat cocked over his ear.
All his life my father wanted to be bold.   10

But the eyes give him away, and the hands
that limply offer the string of dead perch
and the bottle of beer. Father, I love you,
yet how can I say thank you, I who can't hold my
    liquor either
and don't even know the places to fish.   15

The poem is true in its particulars, except that my dad died in 30
June and not October, as the first word of the poem says. I wanted a
word with more than one syllable to it to make it linger a little. But
more than that, I wanted a month appropriate to what I felt at the
time I wrote the poem—a month of short days and failing light,
smoke in the air, things perishing. June was summer nights and days,
graduations, my wedding anniversary, the birthday of one of my
children. June wasn't a month your father died in.

After the service at the funeral home, after we had moved out- 31
side, a woman I didn't know came over to me and said, "He's happier where he is now." I stared at this woman until she moved away.
I still remember the little knob of a hat she was wearing. Then one of
my dad's cousins—I didn't know the man's name—reached out and
took my hand, "We all miss him," he said, and I knew he wasn't saying it just to be polite.

I began to weep for the first time since receiving the news. I had- 32
n't been able to before. I hadn't had the time, for one thing. Now, suddenly, I couldn't stop. I held my wife and wept while she said and did
what she could do to comfort me there in the middle of that summer
afternoon.

I listened to people say consoling things to my mother, and I was 33
glad that my dad's family had turned up, had come to where he was.

I thought I'd remember everything that was said and done that day and maybe find a way to tell it sometime. But I didn't. I forgot it all, or nearly. What I do remember is that I heard our name used a lot that afternoon, my dad's name and mine. But I knew they were talking about my dad. *Raymond*, these people kept saying in their beautiful voices out of my childhood. *Raymond.*

IMELDA

Richard Selzer

I heard the other day that Hugh Franciscus had died. I knew him 1
once. He was the Chief of Plastic Surgery when I was a medical student at Albany Medical College. Dr. Franciscus was the archetype of
the professor of surgery—tall, vigorous, muscular, as precise in his
technique as he was impeccable in his dress. Each day a clean lab coat
monkishly starched, that sort of thing. I doubt that he ever read books.
One book only, that of the human body, took the place of all others. He
never raised his eyes from it. He read it like a printed page as though
he knew that in the calligraphy there just beneath the skin were all the
secrets of the world. Long before it became visible to anyone else, he
could detect the first sign of granulation at the base of a wound, the
first blue line of new epithelium at the periphery that would tell him
that a wound would heal, or the barest hint of necrosis that presaged
failure. This gave him the appearance of a prophet. "This skin graft
will take," he would say, and you must believe beyond all cyanosis,
exudation and inflammation that it would.

He had enemies, of course, who said he was arrogant, that he 2
ex-alted activity for its own sake. Perhaps. But perhaps it was no
more than the honesty of one who knows his own worth. Just look
at a scalpel, after all. What a feeling of sovereignty, megalomania
even, when you know that it is you and you alone who will make
certain use of it. It was said, too, that he was a ladies' man. I don't
know about that. It was all rumor. Besides, I think he had other
things in mind than mere living. Hugh Franciscus was a zealous
hunter. Every fall during the season he drove upstate to hunt deer.
There was a glass-front case in his office where he showed his guns.
How could he shoot a deer? we asked. But he knew better. To us
medical students he was someone heroic, someone made up of several gods, beheld at a distance, and always from a lesser height. If he
had grown accustomed to his miracles, we had not. He had no close
friends on the staff. There was something a little sad in that. As
though once long ago he had been flayed by friendship and now the
slightest breeze would hurt. Confidences resulted in dishonor.
Perhaps the person in whom one confided would scorn him, betray.
Even though he spent his days among those less fortunate, weaker
than he—the sick, after all—Franciscus seemed aware of an air of
personal harshness in his environment to which he reacted by keep-

ing his own counsel, by a certain remoteness. It was what gave him the appearance of being haughty. With the patients he was forthright. All the facts laid out, every question anticipated and answered with specific information. He delivered good news and bad with the same dispassion.

I was a third-year student, just turned onto the wards for the first 3 time, and clerking on Surgery. Everything—the operating room, the morgue, the emergency room, the patients, professors, even the nurses—was terrifying. One picked one's way among the mines and booby traps of the hospital, hoping only to avoid the hemorrhage and perforation of disgrace. The opportunity for humiliation was everywhere.

It all began on Ward Rounds. Dr. Franciscus was demonstrating 4 a cross-leg flap graft he had constructed to cover a large fleshy defect in the leg of a merchant seaman who had injured himself in a fall. The man was from Spain and spoke no English. There had been a comminuted fracture of the femur, much soft tissue damage, necrosis. After weeks of debridement and dressings, the wound had been made ready for grafting. Now the patient was in his fifth postoperative day. What we saw was a thick web of pale blue flesh arising from the man's left thigh, and which had been sutured to the open wound on the right thigh. When the surgeon pressed the pedicle with his finger, it blanched; when he let up, there was a slow return of the violaceous color.

"The circulation is good," Franciscus announced. "It will get bet- 5 ter." In several weeks, we were told, he would divide the tube of flesh at its site of origin, and tailor it to fit the defect to which, by then, it would have grown more solidly. All at once, the webbed man in the bed reached out, and gripping Franciscus by the arm, began to speak rapidly, pointing to his groin and hip. Franciscus stepped back at once to disengage his arm from the patient's grasp.

"Anyone here know Spanish? I didn't get a word of that."   6

"The cast is digging into him up above," I said. "The edges of the 7 plaster are rough. When he moves, they hurt."

Without acknowledging my assistance, Dr. Franciscus took a 8 plaster shears from the dressing cart and with several large snips cut away the rough edges of the cast.

"*Gracias, gracias.*" The man in the bed smiled. But Franciscus had 9 already moved on to the next bed. He seemed to me a man of immense strength and ability, yet without affection for the patients. He did not want to be touched by them. It was less kindness that he showed them than a reassurance that he would never give up, that he would bend every effort. If anyone could, he would solve the problems of their flesh.

Ward Rounds had disbanded and I was halfway down the corri- 10 dor when I heard Dr. Franciscus's voice behind me.

"You speak Spanish." It seemed a command.   11

"I lived in Spain for two years," I told him.   12

"I'm taking a surgical team to Honduras next week to operate on 13 the natives down there. I do it every year for three weeks, somewhere. This year, Honduras. I can arrange the time away from your duties here if you'd like to come along. You will act as interpreter. I'll show you how to use the clinical camera. What you'd see would make it worthwhile."

So it was that, a week later, the envy of my classmates, I 14 joined the mobile surgical unit—surgeons, anesthetists, nurses and equipment—aboard a Military Air Transport plane to spend three weeks performing plastic surgery on people who had been previously selected by an advance team. Honduras. I don't suppose I shall ever see it again. Nor do I especially want to. From the plane it seemed a country made of clay—burnt umber, raw sienna, dry. It had a deadweight quality, as though the ground had no buoyancy, no air sacs through which a breeze might wander. Our destination was Comayagua, a town in the Central Highlands. The town itself was situated on the edge of one of the flatlands that were linked in a network between the granite mountains. Above, all was brown, with only an occasional Spanish cedar tree; below, patches of luxuriant tropical growth. It was a day's bus ride from the airport. For hours, the town kept appearing and disappearing with the convolutions of the road. At last, there it lay before us, panting and exhausted at the bottom of the mountain.

That was all I was to see of the countryside. From then on, there 15 was only the derelict hospital of Comayagua, with the smell of spoiling bana-nas and the accumulated odors of everyone who had been sick there for the last hundred years. Of the two, I much preferred the frank smell of the sick. The heat of the place was incendiary. So hot that, as we stepped from the bus, our own words did not carry through the air, but hung limply at our lips and chins. Just in front of the hospital was a thirsty courtyard where mobs of waiting people squatted or lay in the meager shade, and where, on dry days, a fine dust rose through which untethered goats shouldered. Against the walls of this courtyard, gaunt, dejected men stood, their faces, like their country, preternaturally solemn, leaden. Here no one looked up at the sky. Every head was bent beneath a wide- brimmed straw hat. In the days that followed, from the doorway of the dispensary, I would watch the brown mountains sliding about, drinking the hospital into their shadow as the afternoon grew later and later, flattening us by their very altitude.

The people were mestizos, of mixed Spanish and Indian blood. 16 They had flat, broad, dumb museum feet. At first they seemed to me indistinguishable the one from the other, without animation. All the vitality, the hidden sexuality, was in their black hair. Soon I was to know them by the fissures with which each face was graven. But, even so, compared to us, they were masked, shut away. My job was to follow Dr. Franciscus around, photograph the patients before and after surgery, interpret and generally act as aide-de-camp. It was exhilarating. Within days I had decided that I was not just useful, but essential. Despite that we spent all day in each other's company, there were no overtures of friendship from Dr. Franciscus. He knew my place, and I knew it, too. In the afternoon he examined the patients scheduled for the next day's surgery. I would call out a name from the doorway to the examining room. In the courtyard someone would rise. I would usher the patient in, and nudge him to the examining table where Franciscus stood, always, I thought, on the verge of irritability. I would read aloud the case history, then wait while he carried out his examination. While I took the "before" photographs, Dr. Franciscus would dictate into a tape recorder:

"Ulcerating basal cell carcinoma of the right orbit—six by eight 17 centimeters—involving the right eye and extending into the floor of the orbit. Operative plan: wide excision with enucleation of the eye. Later, bone and skin grafting." The next morning we would be in the operating room where the procedure would be carried out.

We were more than two weeks into our tour of duty—a few days 18 to go—when it happened. Earlier in the day I had caught sight of her through the window of the dispensary. A thin, dark Indian girl about fourteen years old. A figurine, orange-brown, terra-cotta, and still attached to the unshaped clay from which she had been carved. An older, sun-weathered woman stood behind and somewhat to the left of the girl. The mother was short and dumpy. She wore a broad-brimmed hat with a high crown, and a shapeless dress like a cassock. The girl had long, loose black hair. There were tiny gold hoops in her ears. The dress she wore could have been her mother's. Far too big, it hung from her thin shoulders at some risk of slipping down her arms. Even with her in it, the dress was empty, something hanging on the back of a door. Her breasts made only the smallest imprint in the cloth, her hips none at all. All the while, she pressed to her mouth a filthy, pink, balled-up rag as though to stanch a flow or buttress against pain. I knew that what she had come to show us, what we were there to see, was hidden beneath that pink cloth. As I watched, the woman handed down to her a gourd from which the girl drank, lapping like a dog. She was the last patient of the day. They had been waiting in the courtyard for hours.

"Imelda Valdez," I called out. Slowly she rose to her feet, the 19 cloth never leaving her mouth, and followed her mother to the examining-room door. I shooed them in.

"You sit up there on the table," I told her. "Mother, you stand 20 over there, please." I read from the chart:

"This is a fourteen-year-old girl with a complete, unilateral, left- 21 sided cleft lip and cleft palate. No other diseases or congenital defects. Laboratory tests, chest X ray—negative."

"Tell her to take the rag away," said Dr. Franciscus. I did, and the 22 girl shrank back, pressing the cloth all the more firmly.

"Listen, this is silly," said Franciscus. "Tell her I've got to see it. 23 Either she behaves, or send her away."

"Please give me the cloth," I said to the girl as gently as possible. 24 She did not. She could not. Just then, Franciscus reached up and, taking the hand that held the rag, pulled it away with a hard jerk. For an instant the girl's head followed the cloth as it left her face, one arm still upflung against showing. Against all hope, she would hide herself. A moment later, she relaxed and sat still. She seemed to me then like an animal that looks outward at the infinite, at death, without fear, with recognition only.

Set as it was in the center of the girl's face, the defect was utterly 25 hideous—a nude rubbery insect that had fastened there. The upper lip was widely split all the way to the nose. One white tooth perched upon the protruding upper jaw projecting through the hole. Some of the bone seemed to have been gnawed away as well. Above the thing, clear almond eyes and long black hair reflected the light. Below, a slender neck where the pulse trilled visibly. Under our gaze the girl's eyes fell to her lap where her hands lay palms upward, half open. She was a beautiful bird with a crushed beak. And tense with the expectation of more shame.

"Open your mouth," said the surgeon. I translated. She did so, 26 and the surgeon tipped back her head to see inside.

"The palate, too. Complete," he said. There was a long silence. At 27 last he spoke.

"What is your name?" The margins of the wound melted until 28 she herself was being sucked into it.

"Imelda." The syllables leaked through the hole with a slosh and 29
a whistle.

"Tomorrow," said the surgeon, "I will fix your lip. *Mañana*." 30

It seemed to me that Hugh Franciscus, in spite of his years of 31
experience, in spite of all the dreadful things he had seen, must have
been awed by the sight of this girl. I could see it flit across his face for
an instant. Perhaps it was her small act of concealment, that he had
had to demand that she show him the lip, that he had had to force her
to show it to him. Perhaps it was her resistance that intensified the
disfigurement. Had she brought her mouth to him willingly, without
shame, she would have been for him neither more nor less than any
other patient.

He measured the defect with calipers, studied it from different 32
angles, turning her head with a finger at her chin.

"How can it ever be put back together?" I asked. 33

"Take her picture," he said. And to her, "Look straight ahead." 34
Through the eye of the camera she seemed more pitiful than ever, her
humiliation more complete.

"Wait!" The surgeon stopped me. I lowered the camera. A strand 35
of her hair had fallen across her face and found its way to her mouth,
becoming stuck there by saliva. He removed the hair and secured it
behind her ear.

"Go ahead," he ordered. There was the click of the camera. The 36
girl winced.

"Take three more, just in case." 37

When the girl and her mother had left, he took paper and 38
pen and with a few lines drew a remarkable likeness of the girl's
face.

"Look," he said. "If this dot is A, and this one B, this, C, and this, 39
D, the incisions are made A to B, then C to D. CD must equal AB. It
is all equilateral triangles." All well and good, but then came X and
Y and rotation flaps and the rest.

"Do you see?" he asked. 40

"It is confusing," I told him. 41

"It is simply a matter of dropping the upper lip into a normal 42
position, then crossing the gap with two triangular flaps. It is geometry," he said.

"Yes," I said. "Geometry." And relinquished all hope of becom- 43
ing a plastic surgeon.

In the operating room the next morning the anesthesia had 44
already been administered when we arrived from Ward Rounds. The
tube emerging from the girl's mouth was pressed against her lower

lip to be kept out of the field of surgery. Already, a nurse was scrubbing the face which swam in a reddish-brown lather. The tiny gold earrings were included in the scrub. Now and then, one of them gave a brave flash. The face was washed for the last time, and dried. Green towels were placed over the face to hide everything but the mouth and nose. The drapes were applied.

"Calipers!" The surgeon measured, locating the peak of the distorted Cupid's bow. 45

"Marking pen!" He placed the first blue dot at the apex of the 46 bow. The nasal sills were dotted; next, the inferior philtral dimple, the vermilion line. The *A* flap and the *B* flap were outlined. On he worked, peppering the lip and nose, making sense of chaos, realizing the lip that lay waiting in that deep essential pink, that only he could see. The last dot and line were placed. He was ready.

"Scalpel!" He held the knife above the girl's mouth. 47

"O.K. to go ahead?" he asked the anesthetist. 48

"Yes." 49

He lowered the knife. 50

"No! Wait!" The anesthetist's voice was tense, staccato. 51 "Hold it!"

The surgeon's hand was motionless. 52

"What's the matter?" 53

"Something's wrong. I'm not sure. God, she's hot as a pistol. 54 Blood pressure is way up. Pulse one eighty. Get a rectal temperature." A nurse fumbled beneath the drapes. We waited. The nurse retrieved the thermometer.

"One hundred seven . . . no . . . eight." There was disbelief in her 55 voice.

"Malignant hyperthermia," said the anesthetist. "Ice! Ice! Get lots 56 of ice!" I raced out the door, accosted the first nurse I saw.

"Ice!" I shouted. "*Hielo!*[1] Quickly! *Hielo!*" The woman's expres- 57 sion was blank. I ran to another. "*Hielo! Hielo!* For the love of God, ice."

"*Hielo?*" She shrugged. "*Nada.*"[2] I ran back to the operating 58 room.

"There isn't any ice." I reported. Dr. Franciscus had ripped off his 59 rubber gloves and was feeling the skin of the girl's abdomen. Above the mask his eyes were the eyes of a horse in battle.

"The EKG is wild . . ." 60

---

[1] Ice.
[2] Nothing.

"I can't get a pulse . . ."   61

"What the hell . . ."   62

The surgeon reached for the girl's groin. No femoral pulse.   63

"EKG flat. My God! She's dead!"   64

"She can't be."   65

"She is."   66

The surgeon's fingers pressed the groin where there was no   67
pulse to be felt, only his own pulse hammering at the girl's flesh to
be let in.

It was noon, four hours later, when we left the operating room. It   68
was a day so hot and humid I felt steamed open like an envelope. The
woman was sitting on a bench in the courtyard in her dress like a cassock. In one hand she held the piece of cloth the girl had used to con-
ceal her mouth. As we watched, she folded it once neatly, and then
again, smoothing it, cleaning the cloth which might have been the
head of the girl in her lap that she stroked and consoled.

"I'll do the talking here," he said. He would tell her himself, in   69
whatever Spanish he could find. Only if she did not understand was
I to speak for him. I watched him brace himself, set his shoulders.
How could he tell her? I wondered. What? But I knew he would tell
her everything, exactly as it had happened. As much for himself as
for her, he needed to explain. But suppose she screamed, fell to the
ground, attacked him, even? All that hope of love . . . gone. Even in
his discomfort I knew that he was teaching me. The way to do it was
professionally. Now he was standing above her. When the woman
saw that he did not speak, she lifted her eyes and saw what he held
crammed in his mouth to tell her. She knew, and rose to her feet.

"*Señora,*" he began, "I am sorry." All at once he seemed to me   70
shorter than he was, scarcely taller than she. There was a place at the
crown of his head where the hair had grown thin. His lips were
stones. He could hardly move them. The voice dry, dusty.

"No one could have known. Some bad reaction to the medicine for   71
sleeping. It poisoned her. High fever. She did not wake up." The last, a
whisper. The woman studied his lips as though she were deaf. He
tried, but could not control a twitching at the corner of his mouth. He
raised a thumb and forefinger to press something back into his eyes.

"*Muerte,*"[3] the woman announced to herself. Her eyes were   72
human, deadly.

"*Sí, muerte.*" At that moment he was like someone cast, still alive,   73
as an effigy for his own tomb. He closed his eyes. Nor did he open

---

[3] Dead.

them until he felt the touch of the woman's hand on his arm, a touch from which he did not withdraw. Then he looked and saw the grief corroding her face, breaking it down, melting the features so that eyes, nose, mouth ran together in a distortion, like the girl's. For a long time they stood in silence. It seemed to me that minutes passed. At last her face cleared, the features rearranged themselves. She spoke, the words coming slowly to make certain that he understood her. She would go home now. The next day her sons would come for the girl, to take her home for burial. The doctor must not be sad. God has decided. And she was happy now that the harelip had been fixed so that her daughter might go to Heaven without it. Her bare feet retreating were the felted pads of a great bereft animal.

The next morning I did not go to the wards, but stood at the gate 74 leading from the courtyard to the road outside. Two young men in striped ponchos lifted the girl's body wrapped in a straw mat onto the back of a wooden cart. A donkey waited. I had been drawn to this place as one is drawn, inexplicably, to certain scenes of desolation— executions, battlefields. All at once, the woman looked up and saw me. She had taken off her hat. The heavy-hanging coil of her hair made her head seem larger, darker, noble. I pressed some money into her hand.

"For flowers," I said. "A priest." Her cheeks shook as though 75 minutes ago a stone had been dropped into her navel and the ripples were just now reaching her head. I regretted having come to that place.

"Sí, sí," The woman said. Her own face was stitched with flies. 76 "The doctor is one of the angels. He has finished the work of God. My daughter is beautiful."

What could she mean! The lip had not been fixed. The girl had 77 died before he would have done it.

"Only a fine line that God will erase in time," she said. 78

I reached into the cart and lifted a corner of the mat in which the 79 girl had been rolled. Where the cleft had been there was now a fresh line of tiny sutures. The Cupid's bow was delicately shaped, the vermilion border aligned. The flattened nostril had now the same rounded shape as the other one. I let the mat fall over the face of the dead girl, but not before I had seen the touching place where the finest black hairs sprang from the temple.

"Adiós, adiós. . . ." And the cart creaked away to the sound of 80 hooves, a tinkling bell.

There are events in a doctor's life that seem to mark the boundary 81 between youth and age, seeing and perceiving. Like certain dreams, they illuminate a whole lifetime of past behavior. After such an event, a doctor is not the same as he was before. It had seemed to me then to have been the act of someone demented, or at least insanely arrogant. An attempt to reorder events. Her death had come to him out of order. It should have come after the lip had been repaired, not before. He could have told the mother that, no, the lip had not been fixed. But he did not. He said nothing. It had been an act of omission, one of those strange lapses to which all of us are subject and which we live to regret. It must have been then, at that moment, that the knowledge of what he would do appeared to him. The words of the mother had not consoled him; they had hunted him down. He had not done it for her. The dire necessity was his. He would not accept that Imelda had died before he could repair her lip. People who do such things break free from society. They follow their own lonely path. They have a secret which they can never reveal. I must never let on that I knew.

How often I have imagined it. Ten o'clock at night. The hospital of 82 Comayagua is all but dark. Here and there lanterns tilt and skitter up and down the corridors. One of these lamps breaks free from the others and descends the stone steps to the underground room that is the morgue of the hospital. This room wears the expression as if it had waited all night for someone to come. No silence so deep as this place with its cargo of newly dead. Only the slow drip of water over stone. The door closes gassily and clicks shut. The lock is turned. There are four tables, each with a body encased in a paper shroud. There is no mistaking her. She is the smallest. The surgeon takes a knife from his pocket and slits open the paper shroud, that part in which the girl's head is enclosed. The wound seems to be living on long after she has died. Waves of heat emanate from it, blurring his vision. All at once, he turns to peer over his shoulder. He sees nothing, only a wooden crucifix on the wall.

He removes a package of instruments from a satchel and arranges 83 them on a tray. Scalpel, scissors, forceps, needle holder. Sutures and gauze sponges are produced. Stealthy, hunched, engaged, he begins. The dots of blue dye are still there upon her mouth. He raises the scalpel, pauses. A second glance into the darkness. From the wall a small lizard watches and accepts. The first cut is made. A sluggish flow of dark blood appears. He wipes it away with a sponge. No new blood comes to take its place. Again and again he cuts, connecting each of the blue dots until the whole of the zigzag slice is made, first on one side of the cleft, then on the other. Now the edges of the cleft are lined with fresh tissue. He sets down the scalpel and takes up scissors and forceps, undermining the little flaps until each triangle is attached only at one side. He rotates each flap into its new position. He must be certain that they can be swung without tension. They can. He is ready to suture. He fits the tiny curved needle into the jaws of the needle holder. Each suture is placed precisely the same number of millimeters from the cut edge, and the same distance apart. He ties each knot down until the edges are apposed. Not too tightly. These are the most meticulous sutures of his life. He cuts each thread close to the knot. It goes well. The vermilion border with its white skin roll is exactly aligned. One more stitch and the Cupid's bow appears as if by magic. The man's face shines with moisture. Now the nostril is incised around the margin, released, and sutured into a round shape to match its mate. He wipes the blood from the face of the girl with gauze the he has dipped in water. Crumbs of light are scattered on the girl's face. The shroud is folded once more about her. The instruments are handed into the satchel. In a moment the morgue is dark and a lone lantern ascends the stairs and is extinguished.

Six weeks later I was in the darkened amphitheater of the Medical School. Tiers of seats rose in a semicircle above the small stage where Hugh Franciscus stood presenting the case material he had encountered in Honduras. It was the highlight of the year. The hall was filled. The night before he had arranged the slides in the order in which they were to be shown. I was at the controls of the slide projector.

"Next slide!" he would order from time to time in that military voice which had called forth blind obedience from generations of medical students, interns, residents and patients.

"This is a fifty-seven-year-old man with a severe burn contracture of the neck. You will notice the rigid webbing that has fused the chin to the presternal tissues. No motion of the head on the torso is possible. . . . Next slide!"

"Click," went the projector.

"Here he is after the excision of the scar tissue and with the head in full extension for the first time. The defect was then covered. . . . Next slide!"

"Click."

". . . with full-thickness drums of skin taken from the abdomen with the Padgett dermatome. Next slide!"

"Click."

And suddenly there she was, extracted from the shadows, suspended above and beyond all of us like a resurrection. There was the oval face, the long black hair unbraided, the tiny gold hoops in her ears. And that luminous gnawed mouth. The whole of her life seemed to have been summed up in this photograph. A long silence followed that was the surgeon's alone to break. Almost at once, like the anesthetist in the operating room in Comayagua, I knew that something was wrong. It was not that the man would not speak as that he could not. The audience of doctors, nurses and students seemed to have been infected by the black, limitless silence. My own pulse doubled. It was hard to breathe. Why did he not call out for the next slide? Why did he not save himself? Why had he not removed this slide from the ones to be shown? All at once I knew that he had used his camera on her again. I could see the long black shadows of her hair flowing into the darker shadows of the morgue. The sudden blinding flash . . . The next slide would be the one taken in the morgue. He would be exposed.

In the dim light reflected from the slide, I saw him gazing up at 93 her, seeing not the colored photograph, I thought, but the negative of it where the ghost of the girl was. For me, the amphitheater had become Honduras. I saw again that courtyard littered with patients. I could see the dust in the beam of light from the projector. It was then that I knew that she was his measure of perfection and pain— the one lost, the other gained. He, too, had heard the click of the camera, had seen her wince and felt his mercy enlarge. At last he spoke.

"Imelda." It was the one word he had heard her say. At the sound 94 of his voice I removed the next slide from the projector. "Click" . . . and she was gone. "Click" again, and in her place the man with the orbital cancer. For a long moment Franciscus looked up in my direction, on his face an expression that I have given up trying to interpret. Gratitude? Sorrow? It made me think of the gaze of the girl when at last she understood that she must hand over to him the evidence of her body.

"This is a sixty-two-year-old man with a basal cell carcinoma of 95 the temple eroding into the bony orbit . . ." he began as though nothing had happened.

At the end of the hour, even before the lights went on, there was 96 loud applause. I hurried to find him among the departing crowd. I could not. Some weeks went by before I caught sight of him. He seemed vaguely convalescent, as though a fever had taken its toll before burning out.

Hugh Franciscus continued to teach for fifteen years, although 97 he operated a good deal less, then gave it up entirely. It was as though he had grown tired of blood, of always having to be involved with blood, of having to draw it, spill it, wipe it away, stanch it. He was a quieter, softer man, I heard, the ferocity diminished. There were no more expeditions to Honduras or anywhere else.

I, too, have not been entirely free of her. Now and then, in the years that have passed, I see that donkey-cart cortège, or his face bent over hers in the morgue. I would like to have told him what I now know, that his unrealistic act was one of goodness, one of those small, persevering acts done, perhaps, to ward off madness. Like lighting a lamp, boiling water for tea, washing a shirt. But, of course, it's too late now.

BOYHOOD WITH GURDJIEFF

Fritz Peters

The Saturday evening after Gurdjieff's return from America, which had been in the middle of the week, was the first general "assembly" of everyone at the Prieuré,[1] in the study-house. The study-house was a separate building, originally an airplane hangar. There was a linoleum-covered raised stage at one end. Directly in front of the stage there was a small, hexagonal fountain, equipped electrically so that various coloured lights played on the water. The fountain was generally used only during the playing of music on the piano which was to the left of the stage as one faced it.

The main part of the building, from the stage to the entrance at the opposite end, was carpeted with oriental rugs of various sizes, surrounded by a small fence which made a large, rectangular open space. Cushions, covered by fur rugs, surrounded the sides of this rectangle in front of the fence, and it was here that most of the students would normally sit. Behind the fence, at a higher level, were built-up benches, also covered with Oriental rugs, for spectators. Near the entrance of the building there was a small cubicle, raised a few feet from the floor, in which Gurdjieff habitually sat, and above this there was a balcony which was rarely used and then only for "important" guests. The cross-wise beams of the ceiling had painted material nailed to them, and the material hung down in billows, creating a cloud-like effect. It was an impressive interior—with a church-like feeling about it. One had the impression that it would be improper, even when it was empty, to speak above a whisper inside the building.

On that particular Saturday evening, Gurdjieff sat in his accustomed cubicle, Miss Madison sat near him on the floor with her little black book on her lap, and most of the students sat around, inside the fence, on the fur rugs. New arrivals and "spectators" or guests were on the higher benches behind the fence. Mr. Gurdjieff announced that Miss Madison would go over all the "offences" of all the students and that proper "punishments" would be meted out to the offenders. All of the children, and perhaps I, especially, waited with bated breath as Miss Madison read from her book, which seemed to have

---

[1] *Prieuré:* a priory; a large chateau in Fountainebleau, France, where G. I. Gurdjieff conducted his school.

been arranged, not alphabetically, but according to the number of offences committed. As Miss Madison had warned me, I led the list, and the recitation of my crimes and offences was a lengthy one.

Gurdjieff listened impassively, occasionally glancing at one or another of the offenders, sometimes smiling at the recital of a particular misdemeanour, and interrupting Miss Madison only to take down, personally, the actual number of individual black marks. When she had completed her reading, there was a solemn, breathless silence in the room and Gurdjieff said, with a heavy sigh, that we had all created a great burden for him. He said then that he would give out punishments according to the number of offences committed. Naturally, I was the first one to be called. He motioned to me to sit on the floor before him and then had Miss Madison re-read my offences in detail. When she had finished, he asked me if I admitted all of them. I was tempted to refute some of them, at least in part, and to argue extenuating circumstances, but the solemnity of the proceedings and the silence in the room prevented me from doing so. Every word that had been uttered had dropped on the assemblage with the clarity of a bell. I did not have the courage to voice any weak defence that might have come to my mind, and I admitted that the list was accurate.

With another sigh, and shaking his head at me as if he was very much put upon, he reached into his pocket and pulled out an enormous roll of bills. Once again, he enumerated the number of my crimes, and then laboriously peeled off an equal number of notes. I do not remember exactly how much he gave me—I think it was ten francs for each offence—but when he had finished counting, he handed me a sizeable roll of francs. During this process, the entire room practically screamed with silence. There was not a murmur from anyone in the entire group, and I did not even dare to glance in Miss Madison's direction.

When my money had been handed to me, he dismissed me and called up the next offender and went through the same process. As there were a great many of us, and there was not one individual who had not done something, violated some rule during his absence, the process took a long time. When he had gone through the list, he turned to Miss Madison and handed her some small sum—perhaps ten francs, or the equivalent of one "crime" payment—for her, as he put it, "conscientious fulfilment of her obligations as director of the Prieuré."

We were all aghast; we had been taken completely by surprise, of course. But the main thing we all felt was a tremendous compassion for Miss Madison. It seemed to me a senselessly cruel, heartless act against her. I have never known Miss Madison's feelings about this performance; except for blushing furiously when I was paid, she showed no obvious reaction to anything at all, and even thanked him for the pittance he had given her.

The money that I had received amazed me. It was, literally, more 8 money than I had ever had at one time in my life. But it also repelled me. I could not bring myself to do anything with it. It was not until a few days later, one evening when I had been summoned to bring coffee to Gurdjieff's room, that the subject came up again. I had had no private, personal contact with him—in the sense of actually talking to him, for instance—since his return. That evening—he was alone—when I had served him his coffee, he asked me how I was getting along; how I felt. I blurted out my feelings about Miss Madison and about the money that I felt unable to spend.

He laughed at me and said cheerfully that there was no reason 9 why I should not spend the money any way I chose. It was my money, and it was a reward for my activity of the past winter. I said I could not understand why I should have been rewarded for having been dilatory about my jobs and having created only trouble.

Gurdjieff laughed again and told me that I had much to learn.   10

"What you not understand," he said, "is that not everyone can be 11 troublemaker, like you. This important in life—is ingredient, like yeast for making bread. Without trouble, conflict, life become dead. People live in status-quo, live only by habit, automatically, and without conscience. You good for Miss Madison. You irritate Miss Madison all time—more than anyone else, which is why you get most reward. Without you, possibility for Miss Madison's conscience fall asleep. This money should really be reward from Miss Madison, not from me. You help keep Miss Madison alive."

I understood the actual, serious sense in which he meant what he 12 was saying, but I said that I felt sorry for Miss Madison, that it must have been a terrible experience for her when she saw us all receiving those rewards.

He shook his head at me, still laughing. "You not see or under- 13 stand important thing that happen to Miss Madison when give money. How you feel at time? You feel pity for Miss Madison, no? All other people also feel pity for Miss Madison, too."

I agreed that this was so.   14

"People not understand about learning," he went on. "Think 15 necessary talk all time, that learn through mind, through words. Not so. Many things can only learn with feeling, even from sensation. But because man talk all time—use only formulatory centre—people not understand this. What you not see other night in study-house is that Miss Madison have new experience for her. Is poor woman, people not like, people think she funny—they laugh at. But other night, people not laugh. True, Miss Madison feel uncomfortable, feel embarrassed when I give money, feel shame perhaps. But when many people also feel for her sympathy, pity, compassion, even love, she understand this but not right away with mind. She feel, for first time in life, sympathy from many people. She not even know then that she feel this, but her life change; with you, I use you like example, last summer you hate Miss Madison. Now you not hate, you not think funny, you feel sorry. You even like Miss Madison. This good for her even if she not know right away—you will show; you cannot hide this from her, even if wish, cannot hide. So she now have friend, when used to be enemy. This good thing which I do for Miss Madison. I not concerned she understand this now—someday she understand and make her feel warm in heart. This unusual experience—this warm feeling—for such personality as Miss Madison who not have charm, who not friendly in self. Someday, perhaps even soon, she have good feeling because many people feel sorry, feel compassion for her. Someday she even understand what I do and even like me for this. But this kind learning take long time."

I understood him completely and was very moved by his words. 16 But he had not finished.

"Also good thing for you in this," he said. "You young, only boy 17 still, you not care about other people, care for self. I do this to Miss Madison and you think I do bad thing. You feel sorry, you not forget, you think I do bad thing to her. But now you understand not so. Also, good for you, because you feel about other person—you identify with Miss Madison, put self in her place, also regret what you do. Is necessary put self in place of other person if wish understand and help. This good for your conscience, this way is possibility for you learn not hate Miss Madison. All people same—stupid, blind, human. If I do bad thing, this make you learn love other people, not just self."

2

PLACES

MY WOOD

E. M. Forster

A few years ago I wrote a book which dealt in part with the diffi- 1
culties of the English in India. Feeling that they would have had no dif-
ficulties in India themselves, the Americans read the book freely. The
more they read it the better it made them feel, and a cheque to the
author was the result. I bought a wood with the cheque. It is not a large
wood—it contains scarcely any trees, and it is intersected, blast it, by a
public footpath. Still, it is the first property that I have owned, so it is
right that other people should participate in my shame, and should ask
themselves, in accents that will vary in horror, this very important
question: What is the effect of property upon the character? Don't let's
touch economics; the effect of private ownership upon the community
as a whole is another question—a more important question, perhaps,
but another one. Let's keep to psychology. If you own things, what's
their effect on you? What's the effect on me of my wood?

In the first place, it makes me feel heavy. Property does have this 2
effect. Property produces men of weight, and it was a man of weight
who failed to get into the Kingdom of Heaven. He was not wicked,
that unfortunate millionaire in the parable, he was only stout; he stuck
out in front, not to mention behind, and as he wedged himself this
way and that in the crystalline entrance and bruised his well-fed
flanks, he saw beneath him a comparatively slim camel passing
through the eye of a needle and being woven into the robe of God.
The Gospels all through couple stoutness and slowness. They point
out what is perfectly obvious, yet seldom realized: that if you have a
lot of things you cannot move about a lot, that furniture requires dust-
ing, dusters require servants, servants require insurance stamps, and

the whole tangle of them makes you think twice before you accept an invitation to dinner or go for a bathe in the Jordan. Sometimes the Gospels proceed further and say with Tolstoy that property is sinful; they approach the difficult ground of asceticism here, where I cannot follow them. But as to the immediate effects of property on people, they just show straightforward logic. It produces men of weight. Men of weight cannot, by definition, move like the lightning from the East unto the West, and the ascent of a fourteen-stone bishop into a pulpit is thus the exact antithesis of the coming of the Son of Man. My wood makes me feel heavy.

In the second place, it makes me feel it ought to be larger.   3

The other day I heard a twig snap in it. I was annoyed at first, for   4
I thought that someone was blackberrying, and depreciating the value of the undergrowth. On coming nearer, I saw it was not a man who had trodden on the twig and snapped it, but a bird, and I felt pleased. My bird. The bird was not equally pleased. Ignoring the relation between us, it took fright as soon as it saw the shape of my face, and flew straight over the boundary hedge into a field, the property of Mrs. Henessy, where it sat down with a loud squawk. It had become Mrs. Henessy's bird. Something seemed grossly amiss here, something that would not have occurred had the wood been larger. I could not afford to buy Mrs. Henessy out, I dared not murder her, and limitations of this sort beset me on every side. Ahab did not want that vineyard—he only needed it to round off his property, preparatory to plotting a new curve—and all the land around my wood has become necessary to me in order to round off the wood. A boundary protects. But—poor little thing—the boundary ought in its turn to be protected. Noises on the edge of it. Children throw stones. A little more, and then a little more, until we reach the sea. Happy Canute! Happier Alexander! And after all, why should even the world be the limit of possession? A rocket containing a Union Jack, will, it is hoped, be shortly fired at the moon. Mars. Sirius. Beyond which . . . But these immensities ended by saddening me. I could not suppose that my wood was the destined nucleus of universal dominion—it is so very small and contains no mineral wealth beyond the blackberries. Nor was I comforted when Mrs. Henessy's bird took alarm for the second time and flew clean away from us all, under the belief that it belonged to itself.

In the third place, property makes its owner feel that he ought to   5
do something to it. Yet he isn't sure what. A restlessness comes over him, a vague sense that he has a personality to express—the same sense which, without any vagueness, leads the artist to an act of cre-

ation. Sometimes I think I will cut down such trees as remain in the wood, at other times I want to fill up the gaps between them with new trees. Both impulses are pretentious and empty. They are not honest movements towards money-making or beauty. They spring from a foolish desire to express myself and from an inability to enjoy what I have got. Creation, property, enjoyment form a sinister trinity in the human mind. Creation and enjoyment are both very, very good, yet they are often unattainable without a material basis, and at such moments property pushes itself in as a substitute, saying, "Accept me instead—I'm good enough for all three." It is not enough. It is, as Shakespeare said of lust, "The expense of spirit in a waste of shame": it is "Before, a joy proposed; behind, a dream." Yet we don't know how to shun it. It is forced on us by our economic system as the alternative to starvation. It is also forced on us by an internal defect in the soul, by the feeling that in property may lie the germs of self-development and of exquisite or heroic deeds. Our life on earth is, and ought to be, material and carnal. But we have not yet learned to manage our materialism and carnality properly; they are still entangled with the desire for ownership, where (in the words of Dante) "Possession is one with loss."

And this brings us to our fourth and final point: the blackberries. 6

Blackberries are not plentiful in this meager grove, but they are 7 easily seen from the public footpath which traverses it, and all too easily gathered. Foxgloves, too—people will pull up the foxgloves, and ladies of an educational tendency even grub for toadstools to show them on the Monday in class. Other ladies, less educated, roll down the bracken in the arms of their gentlemen friends. There is paper, there are tins. Pray, does my wood belong to me or doesn't it? And, if it does, should I not own it best by allowing no one else to walk there? There is a wood near Lyme Regis, also cursed by a public footpath, where the owner has not hesitated on this point. He had built high stone walls each side of the path, and has spanned it by bridges, so that the public circulate like termites while he gorges on the blackberries unseen. He really does own his wood, this able chap. Dives in Hell did pretty well, but the gulf dividing him from Lazarus could be traversed by vision, and nothing traverses it here. And perhaps I shall come to this in time. I shall wall in and fence out until I really taste the sweets of property. Enormously stout, endlessly avaricious, pseudo-creative, intensely selfish, I shall weave upon my forehead the quadruple crown of possession until those nasty Bolshies come and take it off again and thrust me aside into the outer darkness.

NIAGARA FALLS
William Zinsser

Walden Pond and the Concord writers got me thinking about 1
America's great natural places, and I decided to visit Niagara Falls
and Yellowstone Park next. I had been reminded that one of the most
radical ideas that Emerson and Thoreau and the other Tran-
cendentalists[1] lobbed into the 19th-century American air was that
nature was not an enemy to be feared and repelled, but a spiritual
force that the people of a young nation should embrace and take
nourishment from. The goal, as Thoreau put it in his essay
"Walking," was to become "an inhabitant, or a part and parcel of
Nature, rather than a member of society," and it occurred to me that
the long and powerful hold of Niagara and Yellowstone on the
American imagination had its roots in the gratifying news from
Concord that nature was a prime source of uplift, improvement and
the "higher" feelings.

Niagara Falls existed only in the attic of my mind where collec- 2
tive memory is stored: scraps of songs about honeymooning couples,
vistas by painters who tried to get the plummeting waters to hold
still, film clips of Marilyn Monroe running for her life in *Niagara*,
odds and ends of lore about stuntmen who died going over the falls,
and always, somewhere among the scraps, a boat called *Maid of the
Mist*, which took tourists . . . where? Behind the falls? *Under* the falls?
Death hovered at the edge of the images in my attic, or at least danger. But I had never thought of going to see the place itself. That was
for other people. Now I wanted to be one of those other people.

One misconception I brought to Niagara Falls was that it con- 3
sisted of two sets of falls, which had to be viewed separately. I would
have to see the American falls first and then go over to the Canadian
side to see *their* falls, which, everyone said, were better. But nature
hadn't done anything so officious, as I found when the shuttle bus
from the Buffalo airport stopped and I got out and walked, half running, down a path marked FALLS. The sign was hardly necessary; I
could hear that I was going in the right direction.

Suddenly all the images of a lifetime snapped into place—all the 4
paintings and watercolors and engravings and postcards and calen-

---

[1] *Transcendentalism:* a philosophy emphasizing the intuitive and spiritual above the empirical.

dar lithographs. The river does indeed split into two cataracts, divided by a narrow island called Goat Island, but it was man who put a boundary between them. The eye can easily see them as one spectacle: first the straight line of the American falls, then the island, then the much larger, horseshoe-shaped curve of the Canadian falls. The American falls, 1,060 feet across, are majestic but relatively easy to process—water cascading over a ledge. The Canadian falls, 2,200 feet across, are elusive. Water hurtles over them in such volume that the spray ascends from their circular base as high as the falls themselves, 185 feet, hiding them at the heart of the horseshoe. If the Canadian falls are "better," it's not only because they are twice as big but because they have more mystery, curled in on themselves. Whatever is behind all that spray will remain their secret.

My vantage point for this first glimpse was a promenade that 5 overlooks the falls on the American side—a pleasantly landscaped area that has the feeling of a national park; there was none of the souvenir-stand clutter I expected. My strongest emotion as I stood and tried to absorb the view was that I was very glad to be there. So *that's* what they look like! I stayed at the railing for a long time, enjoying the play of light on the tumbling waters; the colors, though the day was gray, were subtle and satisfying. My thoughts, such as they were, were banal—vaguely pantheistic, poor man's Wordsworth. My fellow sightseers were equally at ease, savoring nature with 19th-century serenity, taking pictures of each other against the cataracts. (More Kodak film is sold here than at any place except the Taj Mahal.) Quite a few of the tourists appeared to be honeymooners; many were parents with children; some were elementary school teachers with their classes. I heard some foreign accents, but on the whole it was—as it always has been—America-on-the-road. The old icon was still worth taking the kids to see. Today more people visit Niagara Falls than ever before: 10 million a year.

Far below, in the gorge where the river reassembles after its dou- 6 ble descent, I saw a small boat bobbing in the turbulent water, its passengers bunched at the railing in blue slickers. Nobody had to tell me it was the *Maid of the Mist*—I heard it calling. I took the elevator down to the edge of the river. Even there, waiting at the dock, I could hardly believe that such a freakish trip was possible—or even prudent. What if the boat capsized? What if its engine stopped? What if . . . ? But when the *Maid of the Mist* arrived, there was no question of not getting on it. I was just one more statistic proving the falls' legendary pull—the force that has beckoned so many daredevils to their death and that compels so many suicides every year to jump.

On the boat, we all got blue raincoats and put them on with due 7
seriousness. The *Maid of the Mist* headed out into the gorge and
immediately sailed past the American falls. Because these falls have
famously fallen apart over the years and dumped large chunks of
rock at their base, the water glances off the rubble and doesn't churn
up as much spray as a straight drop would generate. That gave us a
good view of the falls from a fairly close range and got us only mod-
erately wet.

Next we sailed past Goat Island. There I saw a scene so reminis- 8
cent of a Japanese movie in its gauzy colors and stylized composition
that I could hardly believe it wasn't a Japanese movie. Filtered
through the mist, a straggling line of tourists in yellow raincoats was
threading its way down a series of wooden stairways and catwalks
to reach the rocks in front of the American falls. They were on a tour
called "Cave of the Winds," so named because in the 19th century it
was possible to go behind the falls into various hollowed-out spaces
that have since eroded. Even today nobody gets closer to the falls, or
gets wetter, than these stair people. I watched them as I might watch
a colony of ants: small yellow figures doggedly following a zigzag
trail down a steep embankment to some ordained goal. The sight
took me by surprise and was surprisingly beautiful.

Leaving the ants, we proceeded to the Canadian falls. Until then 9
the *Maid of the Mist* had struck me as a normal excursion boat, the
kind that might take sightseers around Manhattan. Suddenly it
seemed very small. By now we had come within the outer circle of
the horseshoe. On both sides of our boat, inconceivable amounts of
water were rushing over the edge from the height of a 15-story building. I thought of the word I had seen in so many articles about
Niagara's stuntmen: they were going to "conquer" the falls.
Conquer! No such emanations were felt in our crowd. Spray was
pelting our raincoats, and we peered out at each other from inside
our hoods—eternal tourists bonded together by some outlandish
event voluntarily entered into. (Am I really riding down the Grand
Canyon on a burro? Am I really about to be charged by an African
rhino?) The *Maid of the Mist* showed no sign of being afraid of the
Canadian falls; it headed straight into the cloud of spray at the heart
of the horseshoe. How much farther were we going to go? The boat
began to rock in the eddying water. I felt a twinge of fear.

In the 19th-century literature of Niagara Falls, one adjective car- 10
ries much of the baggage: "sublime." Today it's seldom heard, except
in bad Protestant hymns. But for a young nation eager to feel emotions worthy of God's mightiest wonders, the word had a precise

meaning—"a mixture of attraction and terror," as the historian Elizabeth McKinsey puts it. Tracing the theory of sublimity to mid-18th-century aestheticians such as Edmund Burke[2]—in particular, to Burke's *Philosophical Enquiry into the Origin of Our Ideas of the Sublime and Beautiful*—Professor McKinsey says that the experience of early visitors to Niagara Falls called for a word that would go beyond mere awe and fear. "Sublime" was the perfect answer. It denoted "a new capacity to appreciate the beauty and grandeur of potentially terrifying natural objects." Anybody could use it, and everybody did.

Whether I was having sublime feelings as I looked up at the falls 11 I will leave to some other aesthetician. By any name, however, I was thinking: This is an amazing place to be. I wasn't having a 19th-century rapture, but I also wasn't connected in any way to 20th-century thought. I was somewhere in a late-Victorian funk, the kind of romanticism that induced Hudson River School[3] artists to paint a rainbow over Niagara Falls more often than they saw one there. Fortunately, in any group of Americans there will always be one pragmatist to bring us back to earth. Just as I was becoming edgy at the thought of being sucked into the vortex, the man next to me said that he had been measuring our progress by the sides of the gorge and we weren't making any progress at all. Even with its engines at full strength, the *Maid of the Mist* was barely holding its own. That was a sufficiently terrifying piece of news, and when the boat finally made a U-turn I didn't protest. A little sublime goes a long way.

The first *Maid of the Mist* took tourists to the base of the horseshoe 12 falls in 1846. Now, as the mist enveloped our *Maid*, I liked the idea that I was in the same spot and was having what I assume were the same feelings that those travelers had almost 150 years ago. I liked the idea of a tourist attraction so pure that it doesn't have to be tricked out with improvements. The falls don't tug on our sense of history or on our national psyche. They don't have any intellectual content or take their meaning from what was achieved there. They just do what they do.

"When people sit in the front of that boat at the foot of the falls 13 they get a little philosophical," said Christopher M. Glynn, marketing director of the Maid of the Mist Corporation. "They think: There's something bigger than I am that put *this* together. A lot of them have heard about the Seven Wonders of the World, and they ask, 'Is this

---

[2] *Edmund Burke (1729–1797):* an Irish statesman, orator, and writer.
[3] *Hudson River School* artists: a group of 29 nineteenth-century landscape painters in New York state who depicted romantic views of the Catskill Mountains using contrasts of light and dark.

one of them?'" Glynn's father, James V. Glynn, owner and president of the company, which has been owned by only two families since 1889, often has his lunch on the boat and talks with grandfathers and grandmothers who first visited Niagara on their honeymoon. "Usually," he told me, "they only saw the falls from above. Down here it's a totally different perspective, and they find the power of the water almost unbelievable. You're seeing one of God's great works when you're in that horseshoe."

Most Americans come to the falls as a family, said Ray H. Wigle 14 of the Niagara Falls Visitors and Convention Bureau. "They wait until the kids are out of school to visit places like this and the Grand Canyon and Yellowstone. They say, "This is part of your education— to see these stupendous works of nature." On one level today's tourists are conscious of 'the environment,' and they're appreciative of the magnificence of the planet and the fact that something like this has a right to exist by itself—unlike early tourists, who felt that nature was savage and had to be tamed and utilized. But deep down there's still a primal response to uncivilized nature that doesn't change from one century to another. 'I never realized it was like this!' I hear tourists say all the time, and when they turn away from their first look at the falls—when they first connect again with another person—there's always a delighted smile on their face that's universal and childish."

I spent two days at Niagara, looking at the falls at different times 15 of day and night, especially from the Canadian side, where the view of both cataracts across the gorge is the most stunning and—as so many artists have notified us—the most pictorial. Even when I wasn't looking at them, even when I was back in my hotel room, I was aware of them, a low rumble in the brain. They are always *there*. Some part of us, as Americans, has known that for a long time.

Sightseers began coming to Niagara in sizable numbers when the 16 railroads made it easy for them to get there, starting in 1836 with the opening of the Lockport & Niagara Falls line, which brought families traveling on the Erie Canal. Later, workers came over from Rochester on Sunday afternoon after church, and passengers taking Lake Erie steamers came over for a few hours from Buffalo. To stroll in the park beside the falls was an acceptable Victorian thing to do. No other sublime experience of such magnitude was available. People might have heard of the Grand Canyon or the Rockies, but they couldn't get there; vacations were too short and transportation was too slow.

So uplifting were the falls deemed to be that they became a ral- 17
lying point after the Civil War for religious leaders, educators, artists
and scientists eager to preserve them as a sacred grove for the public. This meant wresting them back from the private owners who had
bought the adjacent land from New York State, putting up mills, factories and tawdry souvenir shops, and charging admission for a view
of God's handiwork through holes in the fence. That the state had
sold off its land earlier was not all that surprising; before the Concord
poets and philosophers suggested otherwise, the notion that nature
should be left intact and simply appreciated was alien to the settler
mentality. Land was meant to be cleared, civilized and put to productive use.

Two men in particular inspired the "Free Niagara!" movement: 18
the painter Frederic Edwin Church and the landscape architect
Frederick Law Olmsted,[4] designer of New York's great Central Park.
Church's seven-foot-long *Niagara,* which has been called the greatest
American painting, drew such worshipful throngs when it was first
exhibited in a Broadway showroom in 1857—thousands came every
day—that it was sent on a tour of England, where it was unani-
mously praised by critics, including the sainted John Ruskin.[5] If
America could produce such a work, there was hope for the colonies
after all. Back home, the painting made a triumphal tour of the South
in 1858–59 and was reproduced and widely sold as a chromolitho-
graph. More than any other image, it fixed the falls in the popular
imagination as having powers both divine and patriotic: "an earthly
manifestation of God's attributes" and a prophecy of "the nation's
collective aspirations." Iconhood had arrived; Niagara Falls began to
appear in posters and advertisements as the symbol of America.
Only the Statue of Liberty would dislodge it.

Olmsted, the other man who shaped Niagara's aesthetic, pro- 19
posed the heretical idea of a public park next to the falls and on the
neighboring islands, in which nature would be left alone. This was
counter to the prevailing European concept of a park as a formal
arrangement of paths and plantings. In the 1870s Olmsted and a coali-
tion of zealous Eastern intellectuals launched a campaign of public
meetings, pamphlets, articles and petitions urging state officials to buy

---

[4] *Frederick Edwin Church (1826–1900):* American painter, member of the Hudson River school.
Frederick Law Olmsted (1822–1903): American landscape architect and writer who designed
Central Park in Manhattan and Prospect Park in Brooklyn.
[5] *John Ruskin (1819–1900):* English critic and social theorist.

back the land and raze everything that man had put on it. Massive
political opposition greeted their effort. Not only were the owners of
the land rich and influential; many citizens felt that the government in
a free society had no right to say, "In the public interest we're taking
this land back." The fight lasted 15 years and was narrowly won in
1885 with the creation of the Niagara Reservation, America's first state
park. (One hundred thousand people came on opening day.)
Olmsted's hands-off landscaping, which preserved the natural character of the area and kept essential roads and buildings unobtrusive,
became a model for parks in many other parts of the country.

Gradually, however, the adjacent hotels and commercial enter- 20
prises began to go to seed, as aging resorts will, and in the early 1960s
Mayor E. Dent Lackey of Niagara Falls, New York, decided that only
a sharp upgrading of the American side would enable his city to
attract enough tourists to keep it healthy. Sublimity was no longer the
only option for honeymooners; they could fly to Bermuda as easily
as they could fly to Buffalo. Mayor Lackey, riding the 1960s' almost
religious belief in urban renewal, tore down much of the "falls area."
Like so much '60s renewal, the tearing down far outraced the building back up, but today the new pieces are finally in place: a geologi-
cal museum, an aquarium, a Native American arts and crafts center,
a glass-enclosed botanical garden with 7,000 tropical specimens, an
"Artpark," a shopping mall and other such placid amenities. Even
the new Burger King is tasteful. The emphasis is on history, culture,
education and scenery.

By contrast, over on the Canadian side, a dense thoroughfare 21
called Clifton Hill offers a Circus World, a Ripley's Believe It or Not
Museum, a House of Frankenstein, a Guinness Book of Records
Museum, several wax museums, a Ferris wheel, a miniature golf
course and other such amusements. The result of Mayor Lackey's
faith that Americans still want to feel the higher feelings is that
tourism has increased steadily ever since he got the call.

Niag'ra Falls, I'm falling for you,
Niag'ra Falls, with your rainbow hue,
Oh, the Maid of the Mist
Has never been kissed,
Niag'ra, I'm falling for you.

This terrible song is typical of the objects I found in the local- 22
history section of the Niagara Falls Public Library, along with 20,000
picture postcards, 15,000 stereopticon slides, books by writers as

diverse as Jules Verne and William Dean Howells,[6] and thousands of newspaper and magazine articles. Together, for two centuries, they have sent America the message WISH YOU WERE HERE!, sparing no superlative. Howells, in his novel *Their Wedding Journey*, in 1882, wrote: "As the train stopped, Isabel's heart beat with a child-like exultation, as I believe everyone's heart must who is worthy to arrive at Niagara." Describing the place where Isabel and Basil got off the train as a "sublime destination," Howells says: "Niagara deserves almost to rank with Rome, the metropolis of history and religion; with Venice, the chief city of sentiment and fantasy. In either you are at once made at home by a perception of its greatness . . . and you gratefully accept its sublimity as a fact in no way contrasting with your own insignificance."

What the library gets asked about most often, however, is the 23 "stunts and stunters," according to Donald E. Loker, its local-history specialist. "Just yesterday," he told me, "I got a call from an advertising agency that wanted to use Annie Taylor in an ad campaign." Mrs. Taylor was a schoolteacher who went over the falls in a barrel on October 4, 1901, and survived the plunge, unlike her cat, which she had previously sent over in her barrel for a trial run. Thereby she became the first person to conquer the falls—and also one of the last. Most of the other conquerors tried their luck once too often. Today there is a ban on stunts, but not on ghosts. "Didn't somebody tightrope over this?" is one question that tour guides always get. "People want to see the scene," one of the guides told me. "They want to know: "How did he do it?'"

Of all those glory-seekers, the most glorious was Jean François 24 Gravelet, known as the great Blondin. A Frenchman trained in the European circus, he came to America in 1859 under the promotional arm of P. T. Barnum and announced that he would cross the Niagara gorge on a tightrope on June 30, 1859. "Blondin was too good a showman to make the trip appear easy," Philip Mason writes in a booklet called "Niagara and the Daredevils." "His hesitations and swayings began to build a tension that soon had the huge crowd gripped in suspense." In the middle he stopped, lowered a rope to the *Maid of the Mist*, pulled up a bottle and sat down to have a drink. Continuing toward the Canadian shore, "he paused, steadied the balancing pole and suddenly executed a back somersault. Men screamed, women

---

[6] *William Dean Howells* (1837–1920): introduced realism and naturalism into American literature. *Their Wedding Journey* (1882) was Howell's first novel about a delightful honeymoon to Niagara Falls.

fainted. Those near the rope wept and begged him to come in. . . . For the rest of the fabulous summer of 1859 he continued to provide thrills for the huge crowds that flocked to Niagara to see him. Never content to merely to repeat his last performance, Blondin crossed his rope on a bicycle, walked it blindfolded, pushed a wheelbarrow, cooked an omelet in the center, and made the trip with his hands and feet manacled."

I left the library and went back to the falls for a final look. Far 25 below and far away I saw a tiny boat with a cluster of blue raincoats on its upper deck, vanishing into a tall cloud of mist at the center of the horseshoe falls. Then I didn't see it any more. Would it ever come back out? Historical records going back to 1846 said that it would.

ONCE MORE TO THE LAKE

E. B. White

One summer, along about 1904, my father rented a camp on a lake 1
in Maine and took us all there for the month of August. We all got ring-
worm from some kittens and had to rub Pond's Extract on our arms
and legs night and morning, and my father rolled over in a canoe with
all his clothes on; but outside of that the vacation was a success and
from then on none of us ever thought there was any place in the world
like that lake in Maine. We returned summer after summer—always
on August 1st for one month. I have since become a salt-water man,
but sometimes in summer there are days when the restlessness of the
tides and the fearful cold of the sea water and the incessant wind
which blows across the afternoon and into the evening make me wish
for the placidity of a lake in the woods. A few weeks ago this feeling
got so strong I bought myself a couple of bass hooks and a spinner and
returned to the lake where we used to go, for a week's fishing and to
revisit old haunts.

I took along my son, who had never had any fresh water up his 2
nose and who had seen lily pads only from train windows. On the
journey over to the lake I began to wonder what it would be like. I
wondered how time would have marred this unique, this holy
spot—the coves and streams, the hills that the sun set behind, the
camps and the paths behind the camps. I was sure the tarred road
would have found it out and I wondered in what other ways it
would be desolated. It is strange how much you can remember
about places like that once you allow your mind to return into the
grooves which lead back. You remember one thing, and that suddenly reminds you of another thing. I guess I remembered clearest of
all the early mornings, when the lake was cool and motionless,
remembered how the bedroom smelled of the lumber it was made of
and of the wet woods whose scent entered through the screen. The
partitions in the camp were thin and did not extend clear to the top
of the rooms, and as I was always the first up I would dress softly so
as not to wake the others, and sneak out into the sweet outdoors and
start out in the canoe, keeping close along the shore in the long shadows of the pines. I remembered being very careful never to rub my
paddle against the gunwale for fear of disturbing the stillness of the
cathedral.

The lake had never been what you would call a wild lake. There 3
were cottages sprinkled around the shores, and it was in farming
country although the shores of the lake were quite heavily wooded.
Some of the cottages were owned by nearby farmers, and you would
live at the shore and eat your meals at the farmhouse. That's what
our family did. But although it wasn't wild, it was a fairly large and
undisturbed lake and there were places in it which, to a child at least,
seemed infinitely remote and primeval.

I was right about the tar: it led to within half a mile of the shore. 4
But when I got back there, with my boy, and we settled into a camp
near a farmhouse and into the kind of summertime I had known, I
could tell that it was going to be pretty much the same as it had been
before—I knew it, lying in bed the first morning, smelling the bedroom, and hearing the boy sneak quietly out and go off along the
shore in a boat. I began to sustain the illusion that he was I, and therefore, by simple transposition, that I was my father. This sensation
persisted, kept cropping up all the time we were there. It was not an
entirely new feeling, but in this setting it grew much stronger. I
seemed to be living a dual existence. I would be in the middle of
some simple act, I would be picking up a bait box or laying down a
table fork, or I would be saying something, and suddenly it would be
not I but my father who was saying the words or making the gesture.
It gave me a creepy sensation.

We went fishing the first morning. I felt the same damp moss 5
covering the worms in the bait can, and saw the dragonfly alight on
the tip of my rod as it hovered a few inches from the surface of the
water. It was the arrival of this fly that convinced me beyond any
doubt that everything was as it always had been, that the years were
a mirage and there had been no years. The small waves were the
same, chucking the rowboat under the chin as we fished at anchor,
and the boat was the same boat, the same color green and the ribs
broken in the same places, and under the floor-boards the same
freshwater leavings and débris—the dead helgramite,[1] the wisps of
moss, the rusty discarded fishhook, the dried blood from yesterday's
catch. We stared silently at the tips of our rods, at the dragonflies that
came and went. I lowered the tip of mine into the water, tentatively,
pensively dislodging the fly, which darted two feet away, poised,
darted two feet back, and came to rest again a little farther up the rod.
There had been no years between the ducking of this dragonfly and
the other one—the one that was part of memory. I looked at the boy,

---

[1] The nymph of the May-fly, used as bait.

who was silently watching his fly, and it was my hands that held his rod, my eyes watching. I felt dizzy and didn't know which rod I was at the end of.

We caught two bass, hauling them in briskly as though they were 6 mackerel, pulling them over the side of the boat in a businesslike manner without any landing net, and stunning them with a blow on the back of the head. When we got back for a swim before lunch, the lake was exactly where we had left it, the same number of inches from the dock, and there was only the merest suggestion of a breeze. This seemed an utterly enchanted sea, this lake you could leave to its own devices for a few hours and come back to, and find that it had not stirred, this constant and trustworthy body of water. In the shallows, the dark, water-soaked sticks and twigs, smooth and old, were undulating in clusters on the bottom against the clean ribbed sand, and the track of the mussel was plain. A school of minnows swam by, each minnow with its small individual shadow, doubling the attendance, so clear and sharp in the sunlight. Some of the other campers were in swimming, along the shore, one of them with a cake of soap, and the water felt thin and clear and unsubstantial. Over the years there had been this person with the cake of soap, this cultist, and here he was. There had been no years.

Up to the farmhouse to dinner through the teeming, dusty field, 7 the road under our sneakers was only a two-track road. The middle track was missing, the one with the marks of the hooves and the splotches of dried, flaky manure. There had always been three tracks to choose from in choosing which track to walk in; now the choice was narrowed down to two. For a moment I missed terribly the middle alternative. But the way led past the tennis court, and something about the way it lay there in the sun reassured me; the tape had loosened along the backline, the alleys were green with plantains and other weeds, and the net (installed in June and removed in September) sagged in the dry noon, and the whole place steamed with midday heat and hunger and emptiness. There was a choice of pie for dessert, and one was blueberry and one was apple, and the waitresses were the same country girls, there having been no passage of time, only the illusion of it as in a dropped curtain—the waitresses were still fifteen; their hair had been washed, that was the only difference—they had been to the movies and seen the pretty girls with the clean hair.

Summertime, oh summertime, pattern of life indelible, the fade- 8 proof lake, the woods unshatterable, the pasture with the sweetfern and the juniper forever and ever, summer without end; this was the background, and the life along the shore was the design, the cottagers with their innocent and tranquil design, their tiny docks with the flagpole and the American flag floating against the white clouds in the blue sky, the little paths over the roots of the trees leading from camp to camp and the paths leading back to the outhouses and the can of lime for sprinkling, and at the souvenir counters at the store the miniature birch-bark canoes and the post cards that showed things looking a little better than they looked. This was the American family at play, escaping the city heat, wondering whether the newcomers in the camp at the head of the cove were "common" or "nice," wondering whether it was true that the people who drove up for Sunday dinner at the farmhouse were turned away because there wasn't enough chicken.

It seemed to me, as I kept remembering all this, that those times 9 and those summers had been infinitely precious and worth saving. There had been jollity and peace and goodness. The arriving (at the beginning of August) had been so big a business in itself, at the railway station the farm wagon drawn up, the first smell of the pine-laden air, the first glimpse of the smiling farmer, and the great importance of the trunks and your father's enormous authority in such matters, and the feel of the wagon under you for the long ten-mile haul, and at the top of the last long hill catching the first view of the lake after eleven months of not seeing this cherished body of water. The shouts and cries of the other campers when they saw you, and the trunks to be unpacked, to give up their rich burden. (Arriving was less exciting nowadays, when you sneaked up in your car and parked it under a tree near the camp and took out the bags and in five minutes it was all over, no fuss, no loud wonderful fuss about trunks.)

Peace and goodness and jollity. The only thing that was wrong 10 now, really, was the sound of the place, an unfamiliar nervous sound of the outboard motors. This was the note that jarred, the one thing that would sometimes break the illusion and set the years moving. In those other summertimes all motors were inboard; and when they were at a little distance, the noise they made was a sedative, an ingredient of summer sleep. They were one-cylinder and two-cylinder engines, and some were make-and-break and some were jump-spark,[2] but they all made a sleepy sound across the lake. The one-lungers throbbed and fluttered, and the twin-cylinder ones purred and purred, and that was a quiet sound too. But now the campers all had out-

---

[2] Methods of ignition timing.

boards. In the daytime, in the hot mornings, these motors made a petulant, irritable sound; at night, in the still evening when the afterglow lit the water, they whined about one's ears like mosquitoes. My boy loved our rented outboard, and his great desire was to achieve singlehanded mastery over it, and authority, and he soon learned the trick of choking it a little (but not too much), and the adjustment of the needle valve. Watching him I would remember the things you could do with the old one-cylinder engine with the heavy flywheel, how you could have it eating out of your hand if you got really close to it spiritually. Motor boats in those days didn't have clutches, and you would make a landing by shutting off the motor at the proper time and coasting in with a dead rudder. But there was a way of reversing them, if you learned the trick, by cutting the switch and putting it on again exactly on the final dying revolution of the flywheel, so that it would kick back against compression and begin reversing. Approaching a dock in a strong following breeze, it was difficult to slow up sufficiently by the ordinary coasting method, and if a boy felt he had complete mastery over his motor, he was tempted to keep it running beyond its time and then reverse it a few feet from the dock. It took a cool nerve, because if you threw the switch a twentieth of a second too soon you would catch the flywheel when it still had speed enough to go up past center, and the boat would leap ahead, charging bull-fashion at the dock.

We had a good week at the camp. The bass were biting well and 11 the sun shone endlessly, day after day. We would be tired at night and lie down in the accumulated heat of the little bedrooms after the long hot day and the breeze would stir almost imperceptibly outside and the smell of the swamp drift in through the rusty screens. Sleep would come easily and in the morning the red squirrel would be on the roof, tapping out his gay routine. I kept remembering everything, lying in bed in the mornings—the small steamboat that had a long rounded stern like the lip of a Ubangi, and how quietly she ran on the moonlight sails, when the older boys played their mandolins and the girls sang and we ate doughnuts dipped in sugar, and how sweet the music was on the water in the shining night, and what it had felt like to think about girls then. After breakfast we would go up to the store and the things were in the same place—the minnows in a bottle, the plugs and spinners disarranged and pawed over by the youngsters from the boys' camp, the fig newtons and the Beeman's gum. Outside, the road was tarred and cars stood in front of the store. Inside, all was just as it had always been, except there was more Coca-Cola and not so much Moxie and root beer and birch beer and sarsaparilla. We would walk out with a bottle of pop apiece and sometimes the pop would backfire up our noses and hurt. We explored the streams, quietly, where the turtles slid off the sunny logs and dug their way into the soft bottom; and we lay on the town wharf and fed worms to the tame bass. Everywhere we went I had trouble making out which was I, the one walking at my side, the one walking in my pants.

One afternoon while we were there at that lake a thunderstorm 12 came up. It was like the revival of an old melodrama that I had seen long ago with childish awe. The second-act climax of the drama of the electrical disturbance over a lake in America had not changed in any important respect. This was the big scene, still the big scene. The whole thing was so familiar, the first feeling of oppression and heat and a general air around camp of not wanting to go very far away. In midafternoon (it was all the same) a curious darkening of the sky, and a lull in everything that had made life tick; and then the way the boats suddenly swung the other way at their moorings with the coming of a breeze out of the new quarter, and the premonitory rumble. Then the kettle drum, then the snare, then the bass drum and cymbals, then crackling light against the dark, and the gods grinning and licking their chops in the hills. Afterward the calm, the rain steadily rustling in the calm lake, the return of light and hope and spirits, and the campers running out in joy and relief to go swimming in the rain, their bright cries perpetuating the deathless joke about how they were getting simply drenched, and the children screaming with delight at the new sensation of bathing in the rain, and the joke about getting drenched linking the generations in a strong indestructible chain. And the comedian who waded in carrying an umbrella.

When the others went swimming my son said he was going in 13 too. He pulled his dripping trunks from the line where they had hung all through the shower, and wrung them out. Languidly, and with no thought of going in, I watched him, his hard little body, skinny and bare, saw him wince slightly as he pulled up around his vitals the small, soggy, icy garment. As he buckled the swollen belt suddenly my groin felt the chill of death.

3

ANIMALS

AM I BLUE?

Alice Walker

"Ain't these tears in these eyes tellin' you?"*

For about three years my companion and I rented a small house 1
in the country that stood on the edge of a large meadow that
appeared to run from the end of our deck straight into the mountains. The mountains, however, were quite far away, and between us
and them there was, in fact, a town. It was one of the many pleasant
aspects of the house that you never really were aware of this.

It was a house of many windows, low, wide, nearly floor to ceil- 2
ing in the living room, which faced the meadow, and it was from one
of these that I first saw our closest neighbor, a large white horse, cropping grass, flipping its mane, and ambling about—not over the entire
meadow, which stretched well out of sight of the house, but over the
five or so fenced-in acres that were next to the twenty-odd that we
had rented. I soon learned that the horse, whose name was Blue,
belonged to a man who lived in another town, but was boarded by
our neighbors next door. Occasionally, one of the children; usually a
stocky teen-ager, but sometimes a much younger girl or boy, could be
seen riding Blue. They would appear in the meadow, climb up on his
back, ride furiously for ten or fifteen minutes, then get off, slap Blue
on the flanks, and not be seen again for a month or more.

There were many apple trees in our yard, and one by the fence 3
that Blue could almost reach. We were soon in the habit of feeding
him apples, which he relished, especially because by the middle of

---

summer the meadow grasses—so green and succulent since January—had dried out from lack of rain and Blue stumbled about munching the dried stalks half-heartedly. Sometimes he would stand very still just by the apple tree, and when one of us came out he would whinny, snort loudly, or stamp the ground. This meant, of course: I want an apple.

It was quite wonderful to pick a few apples, or collect those that 4 had fallen to the ground overnight, and patiently hold them, one by one, up to his large, toothy mouth. I remained as thrilled as a child by his flexible dark lips, huge, cubelike teeth that crunched the apples core and all, with such finality, and his high, broad-breasted *enormity*; beside which, I felt small indeed. When I was a child, I used to ride horses, and was especially friendly with one named Nan until the day I was riding and my brother deliberately spooked her and I was thrown, head first, against the trunk of a tree. When I came to, I was in bed and my mother was bending worriedly over me; we silently agreed that perhaps horseback riding was not the safest sport for me. Since then I have walked, and prefer walking to horseback riding—but I had forgotten the depth of feeling one could see in horses' eyes.

I was therefore unprepared for the expression in Blue's. Blue was 5 lonely. Blue was horribly lonely and bored. I was not shocked that this should be the case; five acres to tramp by yourself, endlessly, even in the most beautiful of meadows—and his was—cannot provide many interesting events, and once rainy season turned to dry that was about it. No, I was shocked that I had forgotten that human animals and nonhuman animals can communicate quite well; if we are brought up around animals as children we take this for granted. By the time we are adults we no longer remember. However, the animals have not changed. They are in fact *completed* creations (at least they seem to be, so much more than we) who are not likely *to* change; it is their nature to express themselves. What else are they going to express? And they do. And, generally speaking, they are ignored.

After giving Blue the apples, I would wander back to the house, 6 aware that he was observing me. Were more apples not forthcoming then? Was that to be his sole entertainment for the day? My partner's small son had decided he wanted to learn how to piece a quilt; we worked in silence on our respective squares as I thought . . .

Well, about slavery: about white children, who were raised by 7 black people, who knew their first all-accepting love from black women, and then, when they were twelve or so, were told they must "forget" the deep levels of communication between themselves and "mammy" that they knew. Later they would be able to relate quite calmly, "My old mammy was sold to another good family." "My old mammy was ———— ————." Fill in the blank. Many more years later a white woman would say: "I can't understand these Negroes, these blacks. What do they want? They're so different from us."

And about the Indians, considered to be "like animals" by the 8 "settlers" (a very benign euphemism for what they actually were), who did not understand their description as a compliment.

And about the thousands of American men who marry Japanese, 9 Korean, Filipina, and other non-English-speaking women and of how happy they report they are, *"blissfully,"* until their brides learn to speak English, at which point the marriages tend to fall apart. What then did the men see, when they looked into the eyes of the women they married, before they could speak English? Apparently only their own reflections.

I thought of society's impatience with the young. "Why are they 10 playing the music so loud?" Perhaps the children have listened to much of the music of oppressed people their parents danced to before they were born, with its passionate but soft cries for acceptance and love, and they have wondered why their parents failed to hear.

I do not know how long Blue had inhabited his five beautiful, 11 boring acres before we moved into our house; a year after we had arrived—and had also traveled to other valleys, other cities, other worlds—he was still there.

But then, in our second year at the house, something happened 12 in Blue's life. One morning, looking out the window at the fog that lay like a ribbon over the meadow, I saw another horse, a brown one, at the other end of Blue's field. Blue appeared to be afraid of it, and for several days made no attempt to go near. We went away for a week. When we returned, Blue had decided to make friends and the two horses ambled or galloped along together, and Blue did not come nearly as often to the fence underneath the apple tree.

When he did, bringing his new friend with him, there was a dif- 13 ferent look in his eyes. A look of independence, of self-possession, of inalienable *horse*ness. His friend eventually became pregnant. For months and months there was, it seemed to me, a mutual feeling between me and the horses of justice, of peace. I fed apples to them both. The look in Blue's eyes was one of, unabashed "this is *it*ness."

It did not, however, last forever. One day, after a visit to the city, 14 I went out to give Blue some apples. He stood waiting, or so I thought, though not beneath the tree. When I shook the tree and jumped back from the shower of apples, he made no move. I carried some over to him. He managed to half-crunch one. The rest he let fall to the ground. I dreaded looking into his eyes—because I had of course noticed that Brown, his partner, had gone—but I did look. If I had been born into slavery, and my partner had been sold or killed, my eyes would have looked like that. The children next door explained that Blue's partner had been "put with him" (the same expression that old people used, I had noticed, when speaking of an ancestor during slavery who had been impregnated by her owner) so that they could mate and she conceive. Since that was accomplished, she had been taken back by her owner, who lived somewhere else.

Will she be back? I asked.   15

They didn't know.   16

Blue was like a crazed person. Blue *was*, to me, a crazed person.   17
He galloped furiously, as if he were being ridden, around and around his five beautiful acres. He whinnied until he couldn't. He tore at the ground with his hooves. He butted himself against his single shade tree. He looked always and always toward the road down which his partner had gone. And then, occasionally, when he came up for apples, or I took apples to him, he looked at me. It was a look so piercing, so full of grief, a look so *human*, I almost laughed (I felt too sad to cry) to think there are people who do not know that animals suffer. People like me who have forgotten, and daily forget, all that animals try to tell us. "Everything you do to us will happen to you; we are your teachers, as you are ours. We are one lesson" is essentially it, I think. There are those who never once have even considered animals' rights: those who have been taught that animals actually want to be used and abused by us, as small children "love" to be frightened, or women "love" to be mutilated and raped. . . . They are the great-grandchildren of those who honestly thought, because someone taught them this: "Women can't think," and "niggers can't faint." But most disturbing of all, in Blue's large brown eyes was a new look, more painful than the look of despair: the look of disgust with human beings, with life; the look of hatred. And it was odd what the look of hatred did. It gave him, for the first time, the look of a beast. And what that meant was that he had put up a barrier within to protect himself from further violence; all the apples in the world wouldn't change that fact.

And so Blue remained, a beautiful part of our landscape, very   18
peaceful to look at from the window, white against the grass. Once a friend came to visit and said, looking out on the soothing view: "And it *would* have to be a *white*, horse; the very image of freedom." And I

thought, yes, the animals are forced to become for us merely "images" of what they once so beautifully expressed. And we are used to drinking milk from containers showing "contented" cows, whose real lives we want to hear nothing about, eating eggs and drumsticks from "happy" hens, and munching hamburgers advertised by bulls of integrity who seem to command their fate.

As we talked of freedom and justice one day for all, we sat down 19 to steaks. I am eating misery, I thought, as I took the first bite. And spit it out.

SHOOTING AN ELEPHANT
George Orwell

In Moulmein, in lower Burma, I was hated by large numbers of 1 people—the only time in my life that I have been important enough for this to happen to me. I was sub-divisional police officer of the town, and in an aimless, petty kind of way anti-European feeling was very bitter. No one had the guts to raise a riot, but if a European woman went through the bazaars alone somebody would probably spit betel juice over her dress. As a police officer I was an obvious target and was baited whenever it seemed safe to do so. When a nimble Burman tripped me up on the football field and the referee (another Burman) looked the other way, the crowd yelled with hideous laughter. This happened more than once. In the end the sneering yellow faces of young men that met me everywhere, the insults hooted after me when I was at a safe distance, got badly on my nerves. The young Buddhist priests were the worst of all. There were several thousands of them in the town and none of them seemed to have anything to do except stand on street corners and jeer at Europeans.

All this was perplexing and upsetting. For at that time I had 2 already made up my mind that imperialism was an evil thing and the sooner I chucked up my job and got out of it the better. Theoretically—and secretly, of course—I was all for the Burmese and all against their oppressors, the British. As for the job I was doing, I hated it more bitterly than I can perhaps make clear. In a job like that you see the dirty work of Empire at close quarters. The wretched prisoners huddling in the stinking cages of the lock-ups, the grey, cowed faces of the long-term convicts, the scarred buttocks of the men who had been flogged with bamboos—all these oppressed me with an intolerable sense of guilt. But I could get nothing into perspective. I was young and ill-educated and I had had to think out my problems in the utter silence that is imposed on every Englishman in the East. I did not even know that the British Empire is dying, still less did I know that it is a great deal better than the younger empires that are going to supplant it.[1] All I knew was that I was stuck between my hatred of the empire I served and my rage against the evil-spirited little beasts who tried to make my job impossible. With

---

[1] This essay was written in 1936, three years before the start of World War II; Stalin and Hitler were in power.

one part of my mind I thought of the British Raj[2] as an unbreakable tyranny, as something clamped down, in *saecula saeculorum*,[3] upon the will of prostrate peoples; with another part I thought that the greatest joy in the world would be to drive a bayonet into a Buddhist priest's guts. Feelings like these are the normal by-products of imperialism; ask any Anglo-Indian official, if you can catch him off duty.

One day something happened which in a roundabout way was 3 enlightening. It was a tiny incident in itself, but it gave me a better glimpse than I had had before of the real nature of imperialism—the real motives for which despotic governments act. Early one morning the sub-inspector at a police station the other end of the town rang me up on the phone and said that an elephant was ravaging the bazaar. Would I please come and do something about it? I did not know what I could do, but I wanted to see what was happening and I got on to a pony and started out. I took my rifle, an old .44 Winchester and much too small to kill an elephant, but I thought the noise might be useful in *terrorem*. Various Burmans stopped me on the way and told me about the elephant's doings. It was not, of course, a wild elephant, but a tame one which had gone "must." It had been chained up, as tame elephants always are when their attack of "must"[4] is due, but on the previous night it had broken its chain and escaped. Its mahout,[5] the only person who could manage it when it was in that state, had set out in pursuit, but had taken the wrong direction and was now twelve hours' journey away, and in the morning the elephant had suddenly reappeared in the town. The Burmese population had no weapons and were quite helpless against it. It had already destroyed somebody's bamboo hut, killed a cow, and raided some fruit-stalls and devoured the stock; also it had met the municipal rubbish van and, when the driver jumped out and took to his heels, had turned the van over and inflicted violences upon it.

The Burmese sub-inspector and some Indian constables were 4 waiting for me in the quarter where the elephant had been seen. It was a very poor quarter, a labyrinth of squalid bamboo huts, thatched with palm-leaf, winding all over a steep hillside. I remember that it was a cloudy, stuffy morning at the beginning of the rains. We began questioning the people as to where the elephant had gone and, as usual, failed to get any definite information. That is invariably the case in the

---

[2] Sovereignty.
[3] From time immemorial.
[4] Frenzy.
[5] Keeper.

East; a story always sounds clear enough at a distance, but the nearer you get to the scene of events the vaguer it becomes. Some of the people said that the elephant had gone in one direction, some said that he had gone in another, some professed not even to have heard of any elephant. I had almost made up my mind that the whole story was a pack of lies, when we heard yells a little distance away. There was a loud, scandalized cry of "Go away, child! Go away this instant!" and an old woman with a switch in her hand came round the corner of a hut, violently shooing away a crowd of naked children. Some more women followed, clicking their tongues and exclaiming; evidently there was something that the children ought not to have seen. I rounded the hut and saw a man's dead body sprawling in the mud. He was an Indian, a black Dravidian coolie,[6] almost naked, and he could not have been dead many minutes. The people said that the elephant had come suddenly upon him round the corner of the hut, caught him with its trunk, put its foot on his back, and ground him into the earth. This was the rainy season and the ground was soft, and his face had scored a trench a foot deep and a couple of yards long. He was lying on his belly with arms crucified and head sharply twisted to one side. His face was coated with mud, the eyes wide open, the teeth bared and grinning with an expression of unendurable agony. (Never tell me, by the way, that the dead look peaceful. Most of the corpses I have seen looked devilish.) The friction of the great beast's foot had stripped the skin from his back as neatly as one skins a rabbit. As soon as I saw the dead man I sent an orderly to a friend's house nearby to borrow an elephant rifle. I had already sent back the pony, not wanting it to go mad with fright and throw me if it smelt the elephant.

The orderly came back in a few minutes with a rifle and five cartridges, and meanwhile some Burmans had arrived and told us that the elephant was in the paddy fields below, only a few hundred yards away. As I started forward practically the whole population of the quarter flocked out of the houses and followed me. They had seen the rifle and were all shouting excitedly that I was going to shoot the elephant. They had not shown much interest in the elephant when he was merely ravaging their homes, but it was different now that he was going to be shot. It was a bit of fun to them, as it would be to an English crowd; besides they wanted the meat. It made me vaguely uneasy. I had no intention of shooting the elephant—I had merely sent for the rifle to defend myself if necessary—and it is always unnerving to have a crowd following you. I marched down the hill, looking and

5

---

[6] An unskilled laborer.

feeling a fool, with the rifle over my shoulder and an ever-growing army of people jostling at my heels. At the bottom, when you got away from the huts, there was a metalled road and beyond that a miry waste of paddy fields a thousand yards across, not yet ploughed but soggy from the first rains and dotted with coarse grass. The elephant was standing eight yards from the road, his left side towards us. He took not the slightest notice of the crowd's approach. He was tearing up bunches of grass, beating them against his knees to clean them and stuffing them into his mouth.

I had halted on the road. As soon as I saw the elephant I knew with perfect certainty that I ought not to shoot him. It is a serious matter to shoot a working elephant—it is comparable to destroying a 6 huge and costly piece of machinery—and obviously one ought not to do it if it can possibly be avoided. And at that distance, peacefully eating, the elephant looked no more dangerous than a cow. I thought then and I think now that his attack of "must" was already passing off; in which case he would merely wander harmlessly about until the mahout came back and caught him. Moreover, I did not in the least want to shoot him. I decided that I would watch him for a little while to make sure that he did not turn savage again, and then go home.

But at that moment I glanced round at the crowd that had followed me. It was an immense crowd, two thousand at the least and growing every minute. It blocked the road for a long distance on either 7 side. I looked at the sea of yellow faces above the garish clothes—faces all happy and excited over this bit of fun, all certain that the elephant was going to be shot. They were watching me as they would watch a conjurer about to perform a trick. They did not like me, but with the magical rifle in my hands I was momentarily worth watching. And suddenly I realized that I should have to shoot the elephant after all. The people expected it of me and I had got to do it; I could feel their two thousand wills pressing me forward, irresistibly. And it was at this moment, as I stood there with the rifle in my hands, that I first grasped the hollowness, the futility of the white man's dominion in the East. Here was I, the white man with his gun, standing in front of the unarmed native crowd—seemingly the leading actor of the piece; but in reality I was only an absurd puppet pushed to and fro by the will of those yellow faces behind. I perceived in this moment that when the white man turns tyrant it is his own freedom that he destroys. He becomes a sort of hollow, posing dummy, the conventionalized figure of a sahib.[7] For it is the condition of his rule that he shall spend his life

---

[7] Term used by natives of colonial India when referring to a European of rank.

in trying to impress the "natives," and so in every crisis he has got to do what the "natives" expect of him. He wears a mask, and his face grows to fit it. I had got to shoot the elephant. I had committed myself to doing it when I sent for the rifle. A sahib has got to act like a sahib; he has got to appear resolute, to know his own mind and do definite things. To come all that way, rifle in hand, with two thousand people marching at my heels, and then to trail feebly away, having done nothing—no, that was impossible. The crowd would laugh at me. And my whole life, every white man's life in the East, was one long struggle not to be laughed at.

But I did not want to shoot the elephant. I watched him beating 8 his bunch of grass against his knees, with that preoccupied grand-motherly air that elephants have. It seemed to me that it would be murder to shoot him. At that age I was not squeamish about killing animals, but I had never shot an elephant and never wanted to. (Somehow it always seems worse to kill a *large* animal.) Besides, there was the beast's owner to be considered. Alive, the elephant was worth at least a hundred pounds; dead, he would only be worth the value of his tusks, five pounds, possibly. But I had got to act quickly. I turned to some experienced looking Burmans who had been there when we arrived, and asked them how the elephant had been behaving. They all said the same thing: he took no notice of you if you left him alone, but he might charge if you went too close to him.

It was perfectly clear to me what I ought to do. I ought to walk 9 up to within, say, twenty-five yards of the elephant and test his behavior. If he charged, I could shoot; if he took no notice of me, it would be safe to leave him until the mahout came back. But also I knew that I was going to do no such thing. I was a poor shot with a rifle and the ground was soft mud into which one would sink at every step. If the elephant charged and I missed him, I should have about as much chance as a toad under a steam-roller. But even then I was not thinking particularly of my own skin, only of the watchful yellow faces behind. For at that moment, with the crowd watching me, I was not afraid in the ordinary sense, as I would have been if I had been alone. A white man mustn't be frightened in front of "natives"; and so, in general, he isn't frightened. The sole thought in my mind was that if anything went wrong those two thousand Burmans would see me pursued, caught, trampled on, and reduced to a grinning corpse like that Indian up the hill. And if that happened it was quite probable that some of them would laugh. That would never do. There was only one alternative. I shoved the cartridges into the magazine and lay down on the road to get a better aim.

The crowd grew very still, and a deep, low, happy sigh, as of peo- 10
ple who see the theatre curtain go up at last, breathed from innumer-
able throats. They were going to have their bit of fun after all. The rifle
was a beautiful German thing with cross-hair sights. I did not then
know that in shooting an elephant one would shoot to cut an imagi-
nary bar running from ear-hole to ear-hole. I ought, therefore, as the
elephant was sideways on, to have aimed straight at his ear-hole; actually I aimed several inches in front of this, thinking the brain would be
further forward.

When I pulled the trigger I did not hear the bang or feel the 11
kick—one never does when a shot goes home—but I heard the devilish roar of glee that went up from the crowd. In that instant, in too
short a time, one would have thought, even for the bullet to get there,
a mysterious, terrible change had come over the elephant. He neither
stirred nor fell, but every line of his body had altered. He looked suddenly stricken, shrunken, immensely old, as though the frightful
impact of the bullet had paralysed him without knocking him down.
At last, after what seemed a long time—it might have been five seconds, I dare say—he sagged flabbily to his knees. His mouth slob-
bered. An enormous senility seemed to have settled upon him. One
could have imagined him thousands of years old. I fired again into
the same spot. At the second shot he did not collapse but climbed
with desperate slowness to his feet and stood weakly upright, with
legs sagging and head dropping. I fired a third time. That was the
shot that did for him. You could see the agony of it jolt his whole
body and knock the last remnant of strength from his legs. But in
falling he seemed for a moment to rise, for as his hind legs collapsed
beneath him he seemed to tower upward like a huge rock toppling,
his trunk reaching skywards like a tree. He trumpeted, for the first
and only time. And then down he came, his belly towards me, with
a crash that seemed to shake the ground even where I lay.

I got up. The Burmans were already racing past me across the 12
mud. It was obvious that the elephant would never rise again, but he
was not dead. He was breathing very rhythmically with long rattling
gasps, his great mound of a side painfully rising and falling. His
mouth was wide open—I could see far down into caverns of pale
pink throat. I waited a long time for him to die, but his breathing did
not weaken. Finally I fired my two remaining shots into the spot
where I thought his heart must be. The thick blood welled out of him
like red velvet, but still he did not die. His body did not even jerk
when the shots hit him, the tortured breathing continued without a
pause. He was dying, very slowly and in great agony, but in some

world remote from me where not even a bullet could damage him further. I felt that I had got to put an end to that dreadful noise. It seemed dreadful to see the great beast lying there, powerless to move and yet powerless to die, and not even to be able to finish him. I sent back for my small rifle and poured shot after shot into his heart and down his throat. They seemed to make no impression. The tortured gasps continued as steadily as the ticking of a clock.

In the end I could not stand it any longer and went away. I heard 13 later that it took him half an hour to die. Burmans were bringing dahs[8] and baskets even before I left, and I was told they had stripped his body almost to the bones by the afternoon.

Afterwards, of course, there were endless discussions about the 14 shooting of the elephant. The owner was furious, but he was only an Indian and could do nothing. Besides, legally I had done the right thing, for a mad elephant has to be killed, like a mad dog, if its owner fails to control it. Among the Europeans opinion was divided. The older men said I was right, the younger men said it was a damn shame to shoot an elephant for killing a coolie, because an elephant was worth more than any damn Coringhee coolie. And afterwards I was very glad that the coolie had been killed; it put me legally in the right and it gave me a sufficient pretext for shooting the elephant. I often wondered whether any of the others grasped that I had done it solely to avoid looking a fool.

---

[8] Large knives.

Dog Lab

Claire McCarthy

When I finished college and started medical school, the learning [1]
changed fundamentally. Whereas in college I had been learning
mostly for learning's sake, learning in order to know something, in
medical school I was learning in order to *do* something, do the thing
I wanted to do with my life. It was exhilarating and at the same time
a little scary. My study now carried responsibility.

The most important course in the first year besides Anatomy was [2]
Physiology, the study of the functions and processes of the human
body. It was the most fascinating subject I had ever studied. I found
the intricacies of the way the body works endlessly intriguing and
ingenious: the way the nervous system is designed to differentiate a
sharp touch from a soft one; the way muscles move and work
together to throw a ball; the wisdom of the kidneys, which filter the
blood and let pass out only waste products and extra fluid, keeping
everything else carefully within. It was magical to me that each organ
and system worked so beautifully and in perfect concert with the rest
of the body.

The importance of Physiology didn't lie just in the fact that it was [3]
fascinating, however. The other courses I was taking that semester,
like Histology and Biochemistry, were fascinating, too. But because
Physiology was the study of how the body actually works, it seemed
the most pertinent to becoming a physician. The other courses were
more abstract. Physiology was practical, and I felt that my ability to
master Physiology would be a measure of my ability to be a doctor.

When the second-year students talked about Physiology, they [4]
always mentioned "dog lab." They mentioned it briefly but signifi-
cantly, sharing knowing looks. I gathered that it involved cutting
dogs open and that it was controversial, but that was all I knew. I did-
n't pursue it, I didn't ask questions. That fall I was living day to day,
lecture to lecture, test to test. My life was organized around putting
as much information into my brain as possible, and I didn't pay
much attention to anything else.

I would get up around six, make coffee, and eat my bowl of [5]
cereal while I sat at my desk. There was nowhere else to sit in my dormitory room, and if I was going to sit at my desk, I figured I might as
well study, so I always studied as I ate. I had a small refrigerator and

a hot plate so that I could fix myself meals. After breakfast it was off to a morning of lectures, back to the room at lunchtime for a yogurt or soup and more studying, then afternoon lectures and labs. Before dinner I usually went for a run or a swim; although it was necessary for my sanity and my health, I always felt guilty that I wasn't studying instead. I ate dinner at my desk or with other medical students at the cafeteria in Beth Israel Hospital. We sat among the doctors, staff, and patients, eating our food quickly. Although we would try to talk about movies, current affairs, or other "nonmedical" topics, sooner or later we usually ended up talking about medicine; it was fast becoming our whole life. After dinner it was off to the eerie quiet of the library, where I sat surrounded by my textbooks and notes until I got tired or frustrated, which was usually around ten-thirty. Then I'd go back to the dorm, maybe chat with the other students on my floor, maybe watch television, probably study some more, and then fall asleep so that I could start the routine all over again the next morning.

My life had never been so consuming. Sometimes I felt like a true 6 student in the best sense of the word, wonderfully absorbed in learning; other times I felt like an automaton. I was probably a combination of the two. It bothered me sometimes that this process of teaching me to take care of people was making me live a very study-centered, self-centered life. However, it didn't seem as though I had a choice.

One day at the beginning of a physiology lecture the instructor 7 announced that we would be having a laboratory exercise to study the cardiovascular system, and that dogs would be used. The room was quickly quiet; this was the infamous "dog lab." The point of the exercise, he explained, was to study the heart and blood vessels in vivo,[1] to learn the effects of different conditions and chemicals by seeing them rather than just by reading about them. The dogs would be sedated and the changes in their heart rates, respiratory rates, and blood pressure would be monitored with each experiment. As the last part of the exercise the sleeping dogs' chests would be cut open so we could actually watch the hearts and lungs in action, and then the dogs would be killed, humanely. We would be divided up into teams of four, and each team would work with a teaching assistant. Because so many teaching assistants were required, the class would be divided in half, and the lab would be held on two days.

---

[1] Latin phrase for "in the living being."

The amphitheater buzzed.   8

The lab was optional, the instructor told us. We would not be   9
marked off in any way if we chose not to attend. He leaned against
the side of the podium and said that the way he saw it there was a
spectrum of morality when it came to animal experimentation. The
spectrum, he said, went from mice or rats to species like horses or
apes, and we had to decide at which species we would draw our
lines. He hoped, though, that we would choose to attend. It was an
excellent learning opportunity, and he thought we ought to take
advantage of it. Then he walked behind the podium and started the
day's lecture.

It was all anyone could talk about: should we do dog lab or   10
shouldn't we? We discussed it endlessly.

There were two main camps. One was the "excellent learning   11
opportunity" camp, which insisted that dog lab was the kind of science we came to medical school to do and that learning about the cardiovascular system on a living animal would make it more
understandable and would therefore make us better doctors.

Countering them was the "importance of a life" camp. The   12
extreme members of this camp insisted that it was always wrong to
murder an animal for experimentation. The more moderate members
argued that perhaps animal experimentation was useful in certain
kinds of medical research, but that dog lab was purely an exercise for
our education and didn't warrant the killing of a dog. We could learn
the material in other ways, they said.

On and on the arguments went, with people saying the same   13
things over and over again in every conceivable way. There was
something very important about this decision. Maybe it was because
we were just beginning to figure out how to define ourselves as
physicians—were we scientists, eager for knowledge, or were we
defenders of life? The dog lab seemed to pit one against the other.
Maybe it was because we thought that our lives as physicians were
going to be filled with ethical decisions, and this was our first since
entering medical school. It was very important that we do the right
thing, but the right thing seemed variable and unclear.

I was quiet during these discussions. I didn't want to kill a dog,   14
but I certainly wanted to take advantage of every learning opportunity offered me. And despite the fact that the course instructor had
said our grades wouldn't be affected if we didn't attend the lab, I
wasn't sure I believed him, and I didn't want to take any chances.
Even if he didn't incorporate the lab report into our grades, I was
worried that there would be some reference to it in the final exam,

some sneaky way that he would bring it up. Doing well had become so important that I was afraid to trust anyone; doing well had become more important than anything.

I found myself waiting to see what other people would decide. I was ashamed not to be taking a stand, but I was stuck in a way I'd never been before. I didn't like the idea of doing the lab; it felt wrong. Yet for some reason I was embarrassed that I felt that way, and the lab seemed so important. The more I thought about it, the more confused I became.

Although initially the students had appeared divided more or less evenly between the camps, as the lab day drew nearer the majority chose to participate. The discussions didn't stop, but they were fewer and quieter. The issue seemed to become more private.

I was assigned to the second lab day. My indecision was becoming a decision since I hadn't crossed my name off the list. I can still change my mind, I told myself. I'm not on a team yet, nobody's counting on me to show up. One of my classmates asked me to join his group. I hedged.

The day before group lists had to be handed in, the course instructor made an announcement. It was brief and almost offhand: he said that if any of us wished to help anesthetize the dogs for the lab, we were welcome to do so. He told us where to go and when to be there for each lab day. I wrote the information down.

Somehow, this was what I needed. I made my decision. I would do the lab, but I would go help anesthetize the dogs first.

Helping with the anesthesia, I thought, would be taking full responsibility for what I was doing, something that was very important to me. I was going to *face* what I was doing, see the dogs awake with their tails wagging instead of meeting them asleep and sort of pretending they weren't real. I also thought it might make me feel better to know that the dogs were treated well as they were anesthetized and to be there, helping to do it gently. Maybe in part I thought of it as my penance.

The day of the first lab came. Around five o'clock I went down to the Friday afternoon "happy hour" in the dormitory living room to talk to the students as they came back. They came back singly or in pairs, quiet, looking dazed. They threw down their coats and backpacks and made their way to the beer and soda without talking to anyone. Some, once they had a cup in their hands, seemed to relax and join in conversations; others took their cups and sat alone on the couches. They all looked tired, worn out.

"Well?" I asked several of them. "What was it like?"   22

Most shrugged and said little. A few said that it was interesting   23
and that they'd learned a lot, but they said it without any enthusiasm. Every one of them said it was hard. I thought I heard someone
say that their dog had turned out to be pregnant. Nobody seemed
happy.

The morning of my lab was gray and dreary. I overslept, which I   24
hardly ever do. I got dressed quickly and went across the street to the
back entrance of the lab building. It was quiet and still and a little
dark. The streets were empty except for an occasional cab. I found the
open door and went in.

There was only one other student waiting there, a blond-haired   25
woman named Elise. I didn't know her well. We had friends in common, but we'd never really talked. She was sweet and soft-spoken;
she wore old jeans and plaid flannel shirts and hung out with the
activist crowd. She had always intimidated me. I felt as though I
weren't political enough when I was around her. I was actually a little surprised that she was doing the lab at all, as many of her friends
had chosen not to.

We greeted each other awkwardly, nodding hello and taking our   26
places leaning against the wall. Within a few minutes one of the
teaching assistants came in, said good morning, pulled out some
keys, and let us into a room down the hall. Two more teaching assistants followed shortly.

The teaching assistants let the dogs out of cages, and they ran   27
around the room. They were small dogs; I think they were beagles.
They seemed happy to be out of their cages, and one of them, white
with brown spots, came over to me with his tail wagging. I leaned
over to pet him, and he licked my hand, looking up at me eagerly. I
stood up again quickly.

The teaching assistant who had let us in, a short man with tou-   28
sled brown hair and thick glasses, explained that the dogs were to be
given intramuscular injections of a sedative that would put them to
sleep. During the lab they would be given additional doses intra-
venously as well as other medications to stop them from feeling pain.
We could help, he said, by holding the dogs while they got their
injections. Elise and I nodded.

So we held the dogs, and they got their injections. After a few   29
minutes they started to stumble, and we helped them to the floor. I
remember that Elise petted one of the dogs as he fell asleep and that
she cried. I didn't cry, but I wanted to.

When we were finished, I went back to my room. I sat at my desk, 30 drank my coffee, and read over the lab instructions again. I kept thinking about the dogs running around, about the little white one with the brown spots, and I felt sick. I stared at the instructions without really reading them, looking at my watch every couple of minutes. At five minutes before eight I picked up the papers, put them in my backpack with my books, and left.

The lab was held in a big open room with white walls and lots of 31 windows. The dogs were laid out on separate tables lined up across the room; they were on their backs, tied down. They were all asleep, but some of them moved slightly, and it chilled me.

We walked in slowly and solemnly, putting our coats and back- 32 packs on the rack along the wall and going over to our assigned tables. I started to look for the dog who had licked my hand, but I stopped myself. I didn't want to know where he was.

Our dog was brown and black, with soft floppy ears. His eyes 33 were shut. He looked familiar. We took our places, two on each side of the table, laid out our lab manuals, and began.

The lab took all day. We cut through the dog's skin to find an 34 artery and vein, into which we placed catheters. We injected different drugs and chemicals and watched what happened to the dog's heart rate and blood pressure, carefully recording the results. At the end of the day, when we were done with the experiments, we cut open the dog's chest. We cut through his sternum and pulled open his rib cage. His heart and lungs lay in front of us. The heart was a fist-size muscle that squeezed itself as it beat, pushing blood out. The lungs were white and solid and glistening under the pleura that covered them. The instructor pointed out different blood vessels, like the aorta and the superior vena cava. He showed us the stellate ganglion, which really did look like a star. I think we used the electrical paddles of a defibrillator and shocked the dog's heart into ventricular fibrillation, watching it shiver like Jell-O in front of us. I think that's how we killed them—or maybe it was with a lethal dose of one of the drugs. I'm not sure. It's something I guess I don't want to remember.

Dan was the anesthesiologist, the person assigned to making 35 sure that the dog stayed asleep throughout the entire procedure. Every once in a while Dan would get caught up in the experiment and the dog would start to stir. I would nudge Dan, and he would quickly give more medication. The dog never actually woke up, but every time he moved even the slightest bit, every time I had to think about him being a real dog who was never going to wag his tail or lick anyone's hand again because of us, I got so upset that I couldn't concentrate. In fact, I had trouble concentrating on the lab in general. I kept staring at the dog.

As soon as we were finished, or maybe a couple of minutes before, I left. I grabbed my coat and backpack and ran down the stairs out into the dusk of the late afternoon. It was drizzling, and the medical school looked brown and gray. I walked quickly toward the street.

I was disappointed in the lab and disappointed in myself for doing it. I knew now that doing the lab was wrong. Maybe not wrong for everyone—it was clearly a complicated and individual choice—but wrong for me. The knowledge I had gained wasn't worth the life of a dog to me. I felt very sad.

The drizzle was becoming rain. I slowed down; even though it was cold, the rain felt good. A couple of people walking past me put up their umbrellas. I let the rain fall on me. I wanted to get wet.

From the moment you enter the field of medicine as a medical student, you have an awareness that you have entered something bigger and more important than you are. Doctors are different from other people, we are told implicitly, if not explicitly. Medicine is a way of life, with its own values and guidelines for daily living. They aren't bad values; they include things like the importance of hard work, the pursuit of knowledge, and the preservation of life—at least human life. There's room for individuality and variation, but that's something I realized later, much later. When I started medical school I felt that not only did I have to learn information and skills, I had to become a certain kind of person, too. It was very important to me to learn to do the thing that a doctor would do in a given situation. Since the course instructor, who represented Harvard Medical School to me, had recommended that we do the lab, I figured that a doctor would do it. That wasn't the only reason I went ahead with the lab, but it was a big reason.

The rain started to come down harder and felt less pleasant. I walked more quickly, across Longwood Avenue into Vanderbilt Hall. I could hear familiar voices coming from the living room, but I didn't feel like talking to anyone. I ducked into the stairwell.

I got to my room, locked the door behind me, took off my coat, and lay down on my bed. The rain beat against my window. It was the time I usually went running, but the thought of going back out in the rain didn't appeal to me at all. I was suddenly very tired.

As I lay there I thought about the course instructor's discussion of the spectrum of morality and drawing lines. Maybe it's not a matter of deciding which animals I feel comfortable killing, I thought.

Maybe it's about drawing different kinds of lines: drawing the lines to define how much of myself I will allow to change. I was proud of being a true student, even if it did mean becoming a little like an automaton. But I still needed to be the person I was before; I needed to be able to make some decisions without worrying about what a doctor would do.

I got up off the bed, opened a can of soup, and put it in a pan on 43 the hot plate to warm. I got some bread and cheese out of the refrigerator, sat down at my desk, and opened my Biochemistry text.

Suddenly I stopped. I closed the text, reached over, and turned 44 on the television, which sat on a little plastic table near the desk. There would be time to study later. I was going to watch television, read a newspaper, and call some friends I hadn't called since starting medical school. It was time to make some changes, some changes back.

4

TECHNOLOGY

HOW NOT TO USE THE FAX MACHINE AND THE CELLULAR PHONE

Umberto Eco

The fax machine is truly a great invention. For anyone still unfa- 1
miliar with it, the fax works like this: you insert a letter, you dial the
number of the addressee, and in the space of a few minutes the letter
has reached its destination. And the machine isn't just for letters: it
can send drawings, plans, photographs, pages of complicated figures
impossible to dictate over the telephone. If the letter is going to
Australia, the cost of the transmission is no more than that of an
intercontinental call of the same duration. If the letter is being sent
from Milan to Saronno, it costs no more than a directly dialed call.
And bear in mind that a call from Milan to Paris, in the evening
hours, costs about a thousand lire. In a country like ours, where the
postal system, by definition, doesn't work, the fax machine solves all
your problems. Another thing many people don't know is that you
can buy a fax for your bedroom, or a portable version for travel, at a
reasonable price. Somewhere between a million five and two million
lire. A considerable amount for a toy, but a bargain if your work
requires you to correspond with many people in many different
cities.

Unfortunately, there is one inexorable law of technology, and it is 2
this: when revolutionary inventions become widely accessible, they
cease to be accessible. Technology is inherently democratic, because
it promises the same services to all; but it works only if the rich are
alone in using it. When the poor also adopt technology, it stops working. A train used to take two hours to go from A to B; then the motor
car arrived, which could cover the same distance in one hour. For this

reason cars were very expensive. But as soon as the masses could afford to buy them, the roads became jammed, and the trains started to move faster. Consider how absurd it is for the authorities constantly to urge people to use public transport, in the age of the automobile; but with public transport, by consenting not to belong to the elite, you get where you're going before members of the elite do.

In the case of the automobile, before the point of total collapse 3 was reached, many decades went by. The fax machine, more democratic (in fact, it costs much less than a car), achieved collapse in less than a year. At this point it is faster to send something through the mail. Actually, the fax encourages such postal communications. In the old days, if you lived in Medicine Hat, and you had a son in Brisbane, you wrote him once a week and you telephoned him once a month. Now, with the fax, you can send him, in no time, the snapshot of his newborn niece. The temptation is irresistible. Furthermore, the world is inhabited by people, in an ever-increasing number, who want to tell you something that is of no interest to you: how to choose a smarter investment, how to purchase a given object, how to make them happy by sending them a check, how to fulfill yourself completely by taking part in a conference that will improve your professional status. All of these people, the moment they discover you have a fax, and unfortunately there are now fax directories, will trample one another underfoot in their haste to send you, at modest expense, unrequested messages.

As a result, you will approach your fax machine every morning 4 and find it swamped with messages that have accumulated during the night. Naturally, you throw them away without having read them. But suppose someone close to you wants to inform you that you have inherited ten million dollars from an uncle in America, but on condition that you visit a notary before eight o'clock: if the well-meaning friend finds the line busy, you don't receive the information in time. If someone *has* to get in touch with you, then, he has to do so by mail. The fax is becoming the medium of trivial messages, just as the automobile has become the means of slow travel, for those who have time to waste and want to spend long hours in gridlocked traffic, listening to Mozart or Dire Straits.

Finally, the fax introduces a new element into the dynamics of 5 nuisance. Until today, the bore, if he wanted to irritate you, paid (for the phone call, the postage stamp, the taxi to bring him to your doorbell). But now you contribute to the expense, because you're the one who buys the fax paper.

How can you react? I have already had letterhead printed with   6
the warning "Unsolicited faxes are automatically destroyed," but I
don't think that's enough. If you want my advice, I'd suggest keeping your fax disconnected. If someone has to send you something, he
has to call you first and ask you to connect the machine. Of course,
this can overload the telephone line. It would be best for the person
who has to send a fax to write you first. Then you can answer, "Send
your message via fax Monday at 5.05.27 P.M., Greenwich mean time,
when I will connect the machine for precisely four minutes and
thirty-six seconds."

It is easy to take cheap shots at the owners of cellular phones. But   7
before doing so, you should determine to which of the five following
categories they belong.

First come the handicapped. Even if their handicap is not visible,   8
they are obliged to keep in constant contact with their doctor or the
24-hour medical service. All praise, then, to the technology that has
placed this beneficent instrument at their service. Second come those
who, for serious professional reasons, are required to be on call in
case of emergency (fire chiefs, general practitioners, organ-transplant
specialists always awaiting a fresh corpse, or President Bush, because
if he is ever unavailable, the world falls into the hands of Quayle).
For them the portable phone is a harsh fact of life, endured, but
hardly enjoyed. Third, adulterers. Finally, for the first time in their
lives, they are able to receive messages from their secret lover without the risk that family members, secretaries, or malicious colleagues
will intercept the call. It suffices that the number be known only to
him and her (or to him and him, or to her and her: I can't think of any
other possible combinations). All three categories listed above are
entitled to our respect. Indeed, for the first two we are willing to be
disturbed even while dining in a restaurant, or during a funeral; and
adulterers are very discreet, as a rule.

Two other categories remain. These, in contrast, spell trouble (for   9
us and for themselves as well). The first comprises those persons
who are unable to go anywhere unless they have the possibility of
chattering about frivolous matters with the friends and relations they
have just left. It is hard to make them understand why they should-
n't do it. And finally, if they cannot resist the compulsion to interact,
if they cannot enjoy their moments of solitude and become interested
in what they themselves are doing at that moment, if they cannot
avoid displaying their vacuity and, indeed, make it their trademark,
their emblem, well, the problem must be left to the psychologist.
They irk us, but we must understand their terrible inner emptiness,

be grateful we are not as they are, and forgive them—without, however, gloating over our own superior natures, and thus yielding to the sins of spiritual pride and lack of charity. Recognize them as your suffering neighbor, and turn the other ear.

In the last category (which includes, on the bottom rung of the   10 social ladder, the purchasers of fake portable phones) are those people who wish to show in public that they are greatly in demand, especially for complex business discussions. Their conversations, which we are obliged to overhear in airports, restaurants, or trains, always involve monetary transactions, missing shipments of metal sections, an unpaid bill for a crate of neckties, and other things that, the speaker believes, are very Rockefellerian.

Now, helping to perpetuate the system of class distinctions is an   11 atrocious mechanism ensuring that, thanks to some atavistic proletarian defect, the nouveau riche, even when he earns enormous sums, won't know how to use a fish knife or will hang a plush monkey in the rear window of his Ferrari or put a San Gennaro on the dashboard of his private jet, or (when speaking his native Italian) use English words like "management." Therefore he will not be invited by the Duchesse de Guermantes (and he will rack his brain trying to figure out why not; after all, he has a yacht so long it could almost serve as a bridge across the English Channel).

What these people don't realize is that Rockefeller doesn't need   12 a portable telephone; he has a spacious room full of secretaries so efficient that at the very worst, if his grandfather is dying, the chauffeur comes and whispers something in his ear. The man with power is the man who is not required to answer every call; on the contrary, he is always—as the saying goes—in a meeting. Even at the lowest managerial level, the two symbols of success are a key to the executive washroom and a secretary who asks, "Would you care to leave a message?"

So anyone who flaunts a portable phone as a symbol of power is,   13 on the contrary, announcing to all and sundry his desperate, subaltern position, in which he is obliged to snap to attention, even when making love, if the CEO happens to telephone; he has to pursue creditors day and night to keep his head above water; and he is persecuted by the bank, even at his daughter's First Holy Communion, because of an overdraft. The fact that he uses, ostentatiously, his cellular phone is proof that he doesn't know these things, and it is the confirmation of his social banishment, beyond appeal.

TELEVISION: THE PLUG-IN DRUG

Marie Winn

A quarter of a century after the introduction of television into 1
American society, a period that has seen the medium become so
deeply ingrained in American life that in at least one state the television set has attained the rank of a legal necessity, safe from reposses-
sion in case of debt along with clothes, cooking utensils, and the like,
television viewing has become an inevitable and ordinary part of
daily life. Only in the early years of television did writers and com-
mentators have sufficient perspective to separate the activity of
watching television from the actual content it offers the viewer. In
those early days writers frequently discussed the effects of television
on family life. However, a curious myopia afflicted those early
observers: almost without exception they regarded television as a
favorable, beneficial, indeed, wondrous influence upon the family.

"Television is going to be a real asset in every home where there 2
are children," predicts a writer in 1949.

"Television will take over your way of living and change your 3
children's habits, but this change can be a wonderful improvement,"
claims another commentator.

"No surveys needed, of course, to establish that television has 4
brought the family together in one room," writes the *New York Times*
television critic in 1949.

Each of the early articles about television is invariably accompa- 5
nied by a photograph or illustration showing a family cozily sitting
together before the television set, Sis on Mom's lap, Buddy perched on
the arm of Dad's chair, Dad with his arm around Mom's shoulder.
Who could have guessed that twenty or so years later Mom would be
watching a drama in the kitchen, the kids would be looking at cartoons
in their room, while Dad would be taking in the ball game in the living room?

Of course television sets were enormously expensive in those 6
early days. The idea that by 1975 more than 60 percent of American
families would own two or more sets was preposterous. The splin-
tering of the multiple-set family was something the early writers
could not foresee. Nor did anyone imagine the numbers of hours
children would eventually devote to television, the common use of
television by parents as a child pacifier, the changes television would
effect upon child-rearing methods, the increasing domination of fam-

ily schedules by children's viewing requirements—in short, the *power* of the new medium to dominate family life.

After the first years, as children's consumption of the new medium increased, together with parental concern about the possible effects of so much television viewing, a steady refrain helped to soothe and reassure anxious parents. "Television always enters a pattern of influences that already exist: the home, the peer group, the school, the church and culture generally," write the authors of an early and influential study of television's effects on children. In other words, if the child's home life is all right, parents need not worry about the effects of all that television watching. 7

But television does not merely influence the child; it deeply influences that "pattern of influences" that is meant to ameliorate its effects. Home and family life has changed in important ways since the advent of television. The peer group has become television-oriented, and much of the time children spend together is occupied by television viewing. Culture generally has been transformed by television. Therefore it is improper to assign to television the subsidiary role its many apologists (too often members of the television industry) insist it plays. Television is not merely one of a number of important influences upon today's child. Through the changes it has made in family life, television emerges as *the* important influence in children's lives today. 8

Television's contribution to family life has been an equivocal one. For while it has, indeed, kept the members of the family from dispersing, it has not served to bring them *together.* By its domination of the time families spend together, it destroys the special quality that distinguishes one family from another, a quality that depends to a great extent on what a family *does,* what special rituals, games, recurrent jokes, familiar songs, and shared activities it accumulates. 9

"Like the sorcerer of old," writes Urie Bronfenbrenner, "the television set casts its magic spell, freezing speech and action, turning the living into silent statues so long as the enchantment lasts. The primary danger of the television screen lies not so much in the behavior it produces—although there is danger there—as in the behavior it prevents: the talks, the games, the family festivities and arguments through which much of the child's learning takes place and through which his character is formed. Turning on the television set can turn off the process that transforms children into people." 10

Yet parents have accepted a television-dominated family life so completely that they cannot see how the medium is involved in whatever problems they might be having. A first-grade teacher reports: 11

"I have one child in the group who's an only child. I wanted to   12
find out more about her family life because this little girl was quite
isolated from the group, didn't make friends, so I talked to her
mother. Well, they don't have time to do anything in the evening, the
mother said. The parents come home after picking up the child at the
babysitter's. Then the mother fixes dinner while the child watches
TV. Then they have dinner and the child goes to bed. I said to this
mother. 'Well, couldn't she help you fix dinner? That would be a nice
time for the two of you to talk,' and the mother said, 'Oh, but I'd hate
to have her miss "Zoom." It's such a good program!'"

Even when families make efforts to control television, too often its   13
very presence counterbalances the positive features of family life. A
writer and mother of two boys aged 3 and 7 described her family's
television schedule in an article in the *New York Times*:

> We were in the midst of a full-scale War. Every day was a new
> battle and every program was a major skirmish. We agreed it was a
> bad scene all around and were ready to enter diplomatic negotia-
> tions. . . . In principle we have agreed on 2 1/2 hours of TV a day,
> "Sesame Street," "Electric Company" (with dinner gobbled up in
> between) and two half-hour shows between 7 and 8:30 which
> enables the grown-ups to eat in peace and prevents the two boys
> from destroying one another. Their pre-bedtime choice is dreadful,
> because, as Josh recently admitted, "There's nothing much on I
> really like." So . . . it's "What's My Line" or "To Tell the
> Truth" . . . Clearly there is a need for first-rate children's shows at
> this time. . . .

Consider the "family life" described here: Presumably the father   14
comes home from work during the "Sesame Street"–"Electric
Company" stint. The children are either watching television, gob-
bling their dinner, or both. While the parents eat their dinner in
peaceful privacy, the children watch another hour of television. Then
there is only a half-hour left before bedtime, just enough time for
baths, getting pajamas on, brushing teeth, and so on. The children's
evening is regimented with an almost military precision. They watch
their favorite programs, and when there is "nothing much on I really
like," they watch whatever else is on—because *watching* is the important thing. Their mother does not see anything amiss with watching
programs just for the sake of watching; she only wishes there were
some first-rate children's shows on at those times.

Without conjuring up memories of the Victorian era with family   15
games and long, leisurely meals, and large families, the question
arises: isn't there a better family life available than this dismal, mech-

anized arrangement of children watching television for however long is allowed them, evening after evening?

Of course, families today still do *special* things together at times: go camping in the summer, go to the zoo on a nice Saturday, take various trips and expeditions. But their *ordinary* daily life together is diminished—that sitting around at the dinner table, that spontaneous taking up of an activity, those little games invented by children on the spur of the moment when there is nothing else to do, the scribbling, the chatting, and even the quarreling, all the things that form the fabric of a family, that define a childhood. Instead, the children have their regular schedule of television programs and bedtime, and the parents have their peaceful dinner together.   16

The author of the article in the *Times* notes that "keeping a family sane means mediating between the needs of both children and adults." But surely the needs of adults are being better met than the needs of the children, who are effectively shunted away and rendered untroublesome, while their parents enjoy a life as undemanding as that of any childless couple. In reality, it is those very demands that young children make upon a family that lead to growth, and it is the way parents accede to those demands that builds the relationships upon which the future of the family depends. If the family does not accumulate its backlog of shared experiences, shared *everyday* experiences that occur and recur and change and develop, then it is not likely to survive as anything other than a caretaking institution.   17

Family Rituals

Ritual is defined by sociologists as "that part of family life that the family likes about itself, is proud of and wants formally to continue." Another text notes that "the development of a ritual by a family is an index of the common interest of its members in the family as a group."   18

What has happened to family rituals, those regular, dependable, recurrent happenings that gave members of a family a feeling of *belonging* to a home rather than living in it merely for the sake of convenience, those experiences that act as the adhesive of family unity far more than any material advantages?   19

Mealtime rituals, going-to-bed rituals, illness rituals, holiday rituals, how many of these have survived the inroads of the television set?   20

A young woman who grew up near Chicago reminisces about 21
her childhood and gives an idea of the effects of television upon
family rituals:

"As a child I had millions of relatives around—my parents both 22
come from relatively large families. My father had nine brothers and
sisters. And so every holiday there was this great swoop-down of
aunts, uncles, and millions of cousins. I just remember how wonderful it used to be. These thousands of cousins would come and everyone would play and ultimately, after dinner, all the women would be
in the front of the house, drinking coffee and talking, all the men
would be in the back of the house, drinking and smoking, and all the
kids would be all over the place, playing hide and seek. Christmas
time was particularly nice because everyone always brought all their
toys and games. Our house had a couple of rooms with go-through
closets, so there was always kids running in a great circle route. I
remember it was just wonderful.

"And then all of a sudden one year I remember becoming sud- 23
denly aware of how different everything had become. The kids were
no longer playing Monopoly or Clue or the other games we used to
play together. It was because we had a television set which had been
turned on for a football game. All of that socializing that had gone on
previously had ended. Now everyone was sitting in front of the television set, on a holiday, at a family party! I remember being stunned
by how awful that was. Somehow the television had become more
attractive."

As families have come to spend more and more of their time 24
together engaged in the single activity of television watching, those rituals and pastimes that once gave family life its special quality have
become more and more uncommon. Not since prehistoric times when
cave families hunted, gathered, ate, and slept, with little time remaining to accumulate a culture of any significance, have families been
reduced to such a sameness.

Real People

It is not only the activities that a family might engage in together 25
that are diminished by the powerful presence of television in the
home. The relationships of the family members to each other are also
affected, in both obvious and subtle ways. The hours that the young
child spends in a one-way relationship with television people, an

involvement that allows for no communication or interaction, surely affect his relationships with real-life people.

Studies show the importance of eye-to-eye contact, for instance, 26 in real-life relationships, and indicate that the nature of a person's eye-contact patterns, whether he looks another squarely in the eye or looks to the side or shifts his gaze from side to side, may play a significant role in his success or failure in human relationships. But no eye contact is possible in the child-television relationship, although in certain children's programs people purport to speak directly to the child and the camera fosters this illusion by focusing directly upon the person being filmed. (Mr. Rogers is an example, telling the child "I like you, you're special," etc.) How might such a distortion of real-life relationships affect a child's development of trust, of openness, of an ability to relate well to other *real* people?

Bruno Bettelheim writes: 27

> Children who have been taught, or conditioned, to listen passively most of the day to the warm verbal communications coming from the TV screen, to the deep emotional appeal of the so-called TV personality, are often unable to respond to real persons because they arouse so much less feeling than the skilled actor. Worse, they lose the ability to learn from reality because life experiences are much more complicated than the ones they see on the screen. . . .

A teacher makes a similar observation about her personal view- 28 ing experiences:

"I have trouble mobilizing myself and dealing with real people 29 after watching a few hours of television. It's just hard to make that transition from watching television to a real relationship. I suppose it's because there was no effort necessary while I was watching, and dealing with real people always requires a bit of effort. Imagine, then, how much harder it might be to do the same thing for a small child, particularly one who watches a lot of television every day."

But more obviously damaging to family relationships is the elimi- 30 nation of opportunities to talk, and perhaps more important, to argue, to air grievances, between parents and children and brothers and sisters. Families frequently use television to avoid confronting their problems, problems that will not go away if they are ignored but will only fester and become less easily resolvable as time goes on.

A mother reports: 31

"I find myself, with three children, wanting to turn on the TV set 32
when they're fighting. I really have to struggle not to do it because I
feel that's telling them this is the solution to the quarrel—but it's so
tempting that I often do it."

A family therapist discusses the use of television as an avoidance 33
mechanism:

"In a family I know the father comes home from work and turns 34
on the television set. The children come and watch with him and the
wife serves them their meal in front of the set. He then goes and takes
a shower, or works on the car or something. She then goes and has her
own dinner in front of the television set. It's a symptom of a
deeper-rooted problem, sure. But it would help them all to get rid of .
the set. It would be far easier to work on what the symptom really
means without the television. The television simply encourages a double avoidance of each other. They'd find out more quickly what was
going on if they weren't able to hide behind the TV. Things wouldn't
necessarily be better, of course, but they wouldn't be anesthetized."

The decreased opportunities for simple conversation between 35
parents and children in the television-centered home may help explain
an observation made by an emergency room nurse at a Boston hospital. She reports that parents just seem to sit there these days when they
come in with a sick or seriously injured child, although talking to the
child would distract and comfort him. "They don't seem to know *how*
to talk to their own children at any length," the nurse observes.
Similarly, a television critic writes in the *New York Times:* "I had just a
day ago taken my son to the emergency ward of a hospital for stitches
above his left eye, and the occasion seemed no more real to me than
Maalot or 54th Street, south-central Los Angeles. There was distance
and numbness and an inability to turn off the total institution. I didn't
behave at all; I just watched. . . ."

A number of research studies substantiate the assumption that 36
television interferes with family activities and the formation of family
relationships. One survey shows that 78 percent of the respondents
indicated no conversation taking place during viewing except at
specified times such as commercials. The study notes: "The television
atmosphere in most households is one of quiet absorption on the part
of family members who are present. The nature of the family social
life during a program could be described as 'parallel' rather than
interactive, and the set does seem to dominate family life when it is
on." Thirty-six percent of the respondents in another study indicated
that television viewing was the only family activity participated in
during the week.

In a summary of research findings on television's effect on fam- 37
ily interactions James Gabardino states: "The early findings suggest
that television had a disruptive effect upon interaction and thus
presumably human development. . . . It is not unreasonable to ask:
'Is the fact that the average American family during the 1950s came
to include two parents, two children and a television set somehow
related to the psychosocial characteristics of the young adults of the
1970s?'"

Undermining the Family

In its effect on family relationships, in its facilitation of parental 38
withdrawal from an active role in the socialization of their children,
and in its replacement of family rituals and special events, television
has played an important role in the disintegration of the American
family. But of course it has not been the only contributing factor, perhaps not even the most important one. The steadily rising divorce
rate, the increase in the number of working mothers, the decline of
the extended family, the breakdown of neighborhoods and communities, the growing isolation of the nuclear family—all have seriously
affected the family.

As Urie Bronfenbrenner suggests, the sources of family break- 39
down do not come from the family itself, but from the circumstances
in which the family finds itself and the way of life imposed upon it
by those circumstances. "When those circumstances and the way of
life they generate undermine relationships of trust and emotional
security between family members, when they make it difficult for
parents to care for, educate and enjoy their children, when there is
no support or recognition from the outside world for one's role as a
parent and when time spent with one's family means frustration of
career, personal fulfillment and peace of mind, then the development of the child is adversely affected," he writes.

But while the roots of alienation go deep into the fabric of 40
American social history, television's presence in the home fertilizes
them, encourages their wild and unchecked growth. Perhaps it is
true that America's commitment to the television experience masks a
spiritual vacuum, an empty and barren way of life, a desert of materialism. But it is television's dominant role in the family that anes-
thetizes the family into accepting its unhappy state and prevents it
from struggling to better its condition, to improve its relationships,
and to regain some of the richness it once possessed.

Others have noted the role of mass media in perpetuating an 41
unsatisfactory *status quo.* Leisure-time activity, writes Irving Howe,
"must provide relief from work monotony without making the return
to work too unbearable; it must provide amusement without insight
and pleasure without disturbance—as distinct from art which gives
pleasure through disturbance. Mass culture is thus oriented towards
a central aspect of industrial society: the depersonalization of the individual." Similarly, Jacques Ellul rejects the idea that television is a
legitimate means of educating the citizen: "Education . . . takes
place only incidentally. The clouding of his consciousness is
paramount. . . ."

And so the American family muddles on, dimly aware that 42
something is amiss but distracted from an understanding of its
plight by an endless stream of television images. As family ties grow
weaker and vaguer, as children's lives become more separate from
their parents', as parents' educational role in their children's lives is
taken over by television and schools, family life becomes increasingly more unsatisfying for both parents and children. All that
seems to be left is Love, an abstraction that family members *know* is
necessary but find great difficulty giving each other because the traditional opportunities for expressing love within the family have
been reduced or destroyed.

For contemporary parents, love toward each other has increas- 43
ingly come to mean successful sexual relations, as witnessed by the
proliferation of sex manuals and sex therapists. The opportunities for
manifesting other forms of love through mutual support, understanding, nurturing, even, to use an unpopular word, serving each other, are
less and less available as mothers and fathers seek their independent
destinies outside the family.

As for love of children, this love is increasingly expressed 44
through supplying material comforts, amusements, and educational
opportunities. Parents show their love for their children by sending
them to good schools and camps, by providing them with good food
and good doctors, by buying them toys, books , games, and a television set of their very own. Parents will even go further and express
their love by attending PTA meetings to improve their children's
schools, or by joining groups that are acting to improve the quality of
their children's television programs.

But this is love at a remove, and is rarely understood by children. 45
The more direct forms of parental love require time and patience,
steady, dependable, ungrudgingly given time actually spent *with* a
child, reading to him, comforting him, playing, joking, and working

with him. But even if a parent were eager and willing to demonstrate that sort of direct love to his children today, the opportunities are diminished. What with school and Little League and piano lessons and, of course, the inevitable television programs, a day seems to offer just enough time for a good-night kiss.

CYBERHOOD VS. NEIGHBORHOOD

John Perry Barlow

"There is no there there."

— Gertrude Stein (speaking of (Oakland)

"It ain't no Amish barn-raising in there . . ."

— Bruce Sterling (speaking of cyberspace)

I am often asked how I went from pushing cows around a 1
remote Wyoming ranch to my present occupation (which *Wall Street
Journal* recently described as "cyberspace cadet"). I haven't got a
short answer, but I suppose I came to the virtual world looking for
community.

Unlike most modern Americans, I grew up in an actual place, an 2
entire nonintentional community called Pinedale, Wyoming. As I
struggled for nearly a generation to keep my ranch in the family, I
was motivated by the belief that such places were the spiritual home
of humanity. But I knew their future was not promising.

At the dawn of the 20th century, over 40 percent of the American 3
workforce lived off the land. The majority of us lived in towns like
Pinedale. Now fewer than 1 percent of us extract a living from the
soil. We just became too productive for our own good.

Of course, the population followed the jobs. Farming and ranch- 4
ing communities are now home to a demographically insignificant
percentage of Americans, the vast majority of whom live not in ranch
houses but in more or less identical split level "ranch homes" in more
or less identical suburban "communities." Generica.

In my view, these are neither communities nor homes. I believe 5
the combination of television and suburban population patterns is
simply toxic to the soul. I see much evidence in contemporary
America to support this view.

Meanwhile, back at the ranch, doom impended. And, as I 6
watched the community in Pinedale growing ill from the same economic forces that were killing my family's ranch, the Bar Cross, satellite dishes brought the cultural infection of television. I started
looking around for evidence that community in America would not
perish altogether.

I took some heart in the mysterious nomadic City of the 7
Deadheads, the virtually physical town that follows the Grateful

Dead around the country. The Deadheads lacked place, touching down briefly wherever the band happened to be playing, and they lacked continuity in time, since they had to suffer a new diaspora every time the band moved on or went home. But they had many of the other necessary elements of community, including a culture, a religion of sorts (which, though it lacked dogma, had most of the other, more nurturing aspects of spiritual practice), a sense of necessity, and most importantly, shared adversity.

I wanted to know more about the flavor of their interaction, what 8 they thought and felt, but since I wrote Dead songs (including "Estimated Prophet" and "Cassidy"), I was a minor icon to the Deadheads, and was thus inhibited, in some socially Heisenbergian way, from getting a clear view of what really went on among them.

Then, in 1987, I heard about a "place" where Deadheads gath- 9 ered where I could move among them without distorting too much the field of observation. Better, this was a place I could visit without leaving Wyoming. It was a shared computer in Sausalito, California, called the Whole Earth 'Lectronic Link, or WELL. After a lot of struggling with modems, serial cables, init strings, and other Computer arcana that seemed utterly out of phase with such notions as Deadheads and small towns, I found myself looking at the glowing yellow word "Login:" beyond which lay my future.

"Inside" the WELL were Deadheads in community. There were 10 thousands of them there, gossiping, complaining (mostly about the Grateful Dead), comforting and harassing each other, bartering, engaging in religion (or at least exchanging their totemic set lists), beginning and ending love affairs, praying for one another's sick kids. There was, it seemed, everything one might find going on in a small town, save dragging Main Street and making out on the back roads.

I was delighted. I felt I had found the new locale of human com- 11 munity—never mind that the whole thing was being conducted in mere words by minds from whom the bodies had been amputated. Never mind that all these people were deaf, dumb, and blind as paramecia or that their town had neither seasons nor sunsets nor smells.

Surely all these deficiencies would be remedied by richer, faster 12 communications media. The featureless log-in handles would gradually acquire video faces (and thus expressions), shaded 3-D body puppets (and thus body language). This "space" which I recognized at once to be a primitive form of the cyberspace William Gibson predicted in his sci-fi novel *Neuromancer*, was still without apparent dimensions of vistas. But virtual reality would change all that in time.

Meanwhile, the commons, or something like it, had been redis- 13
covered. Once again, people from the 'burbs had a place where they
could encounter their friends as my fellow Pinedalians did at the
post office and the Wrangler Cafe. They had a place where their
hearts could remain as the companies they worked for shuffled their
bodies around America. They could put down roots that could not be
ripped out by forces of economic history. They had a collective stake.
They had a community.

It is seven years now since I discovered the WELL. In that time, I co- 14
founded an organization, the Electronic Frontier Foundation, dedicated to protecting its interests and those of other virtual
communities like it from raids by physical government. I've spent
countless hours typing away at its residents, and I've watched the
larger context that contains it, the Internet, grow at such an explosive
rate that, by 2004, every human on the planet will have an e-mail
address unless the growth curve flattens (which it will).

My enthusiasm for virtuality has cooled. In fact, unless one 15
counts interaction with the rather too large society of those with
whom I exchange electronic mail, I don't spend much time engaging
in virtual community, at all. Many of the near-term benefits I anticipated from it seem to remain as far in the future as they did when I
first logged in. Perhaps they always will.

Pinedale works, more or less, as it is, but a lot is still missing from 16
the communities of cyberspace, whether they be places like the
WELL, the fractious newsgroups of USENET, the silent "auditori-
ums" of America Online, or even enclaves on the promising World
Wide Web.

What is missing? Well, to quote Ranjit Makkuni of Xerox 17
Corporation's Palo Alto Research Center, "the *prāna* is missing,"
prāna being the Hindu term for both breath and spirit. I think he is
right about this and that perhaps the central question of the virtual
age is whether or not *prāna* can somehow be made to fit through any
disembodied medium.

Prāna is, to my mind, the literally vital element in the holy and 18
unseen ecology of relationship, the dense mesh of invisible life, on
whose surface carbon-based life floats like a thin film. It is at the heart
of the fundamental and profound difference between information
and experience. Jaron Lanier has said that "information is alienated
experience," and, that being true, *prāna* is part of what is removed
when you create such easily transmissible replicas of experience as,
say, the evening news.

Obviously a great many other, less spiritual, things are also miss- 19
ing entirely, like body language, sex, death, tone of voice, clothing,
beauty (or homeliness), weather, violence, vegetation, wildlife, pets,
architecture, music, smells, sunlight, and that ol' harvest moon. In
short, most of the things that make my life real to me.

Present, but in far less abundance than in the physical world, 20
which I call "meat space," are women, children, old people, poor
people, and the genuinely blind. Also mostly missing are the illiter-
ate and the continent of Africa. There is not much human diversity in
cyberspace, which is populated, as near as I can tell, by white males
under 50 with plenty of computer terminal time, great typing skills,
high math SATs, strongly held opinions on just about everything, and
an excruciating face-to-face shyness, especially with the opposite sex.

But diversity is as essential to healthy community as it is to 21
healthy ecosystems (which are, in my view, different from communities only in unimportant aspects).

I believe that the principal reason for the almost universal failure 22
of the intentional communities of the '60s and '70s was a lack of
diversity in their members. It was a rare commune with any old people in it, or people who were fundamentally out of philosophical
agreement with the majority.

Indeed, it is the usual problem when we try to build something 23
that can only be grown. Natural systems, such as human communities, are simply too complex to design by the engineering principles
we insist on applying to them. Like Dr. Frankenstein, western civi-
lization is now finding its rational skills inadequate to the task of creating and caring for life. We would do better to return to a kind of
agricultural mind-set in which we humbly try to re-create the conditions from which life has sprung before. And leave the rest to God.

Given that it has been built so far almost entirely by people with 24
engineering degrees, it is not so surprising that cyberspace has the
kind of overdesigned quality that leaves out all kinds of elements
nature would have provided invisibly.

Also missing from both the communes of the '60s and from 25
cyberspace are a couple of elements that I believe are very important,
if not essential, to the formation and preservation of a real community: an absence of alternatives and a sense of genuine adversity, generally shared. What about these?

It is hard to argue that anyone would find losing a modem liter- 26
ally hard to survive, while many have remained in small towns,
have tolerated their intolerances and created entertainment to
enliven their culturally arid lives simply because it seemed there

was no choice but to stay. There are many investments—spiritual, material, and temporal—one is willing to put into a home one cannot leave. Communities are often the beneficiaries of these involuntary investments.

But when the going gets rough in cyberspace, it is even easier to 27 move than it is in the burbs, where, given the fact that the average American moves some 12 times in his or her life, moving appears to be pretty easy. You cannot only find another bulletin board service (BBS) or newsgroup to hang out in; you can, with very little effort, start your own.

And then there is the bond of joint suffering. Most community is 28 a cultural stockade erected against a common enemy that can take many forms. In Pinedale, we bore together, with an understanding needing little expression, the fact that Upper Green River Valley is the coldest spot, as measured by annual mean temperature, in the lower 48 states. We knew that if somebody was stopped on the road most winter nights, he would probably die there, so the fact that we might loathe him was not sufficient reason to drive on past his broken pickup.

By the same token, the Deadheads have the Drug Enforcement 29 Administration, which strives to give them 20-year prison terms without parole for distributing the fairly harmless sacrament of their faith. They have an additional bond in the fact that when their Microbuses die, as they often do, no one but another Deadhead is likely to stop to help them.

But what are the shared adversities of cyberspace? Lousy user 30 interfaces? The flames of harsh invective? Dumb jokes? Surely these can all be survived without the sanctuary provided by fellow sufferers.

One is always free to yank the jack, as I have mostly done. For 31 me, the physical world offers far more opportunity for *prāna* rich connections with my fellow creatures. Even for someone whose body is in a state of perpetual motion, I feel I can generally find more community among the still-embodied.

Finally, there is that shyness factor. Not only are we trying to 32 build community here among people who have never experienced any in my sense of the term, we are trying to build community among people who, in their lives, have rarely used the word *we* in a heartfelt way. It is a vast club, and many of the members—following Groucho Marx—wouldn't want to join a club that would have them.

And yet . . . 33

How quickly physical community continues to deteriorate. Even 34 Pinedale, which seems to have survived the plague of ranch failures, feels increasingly cut off from itself. Many of the ranches are now owned by corporate types who fly their Gulfstreams in to fish and are rarely around during the many months when the creeks are frozen over and neighbors are needed. They have kept the ranches alive financially, but they actively discourage their managers from the interdependence my former colleagues and I require. They keep agriculture on life support, still alive but lacking a functional heart.

And the town has been inundated with suburbanites who flee 35 here, bringing all their terrors and suspicions with them. They spend their evenings as they did in Orange County, watching television or socializing in hermetic little enclaves of fundamentalist Christianity that seem to separate them from us and even, given their sectarian animosities, from one another. The town remains. The community is largely a wraith of nostalgia.

So where else can we look for the connection we need to prevent 36 our plunging further into the condition of separateness Nietzsche called sin? What is there to do but to dive further into the bramble bush of information that, in its broadest forms, has done so much to tear us apart?

Cyberspace, for all its current deficiencies and failed promises, is 37 not without some very real solace already.

Some months ago, the great love of my life, a vivid young 38 woman with whom I intended to spend the rest of it, dropped dead of undiagnosed viral cardiomyopathy two days short of her 30th birthday. I felt as if my own heart had been as shredded as hers.

We had lived together in New York City. Except for my daugh- 39 ters, no one from Pinedale had met her. I needed a community to wrap around myself against colder winds than fortune had ever blown at me before. And without looking, I found I had one in the virtual world.

On the WELL, there was a topic announcing her death in one of 40 the conferences to which I posted the eulogy I had read over her before burying her in her own small town of Nanaimo, British Columbia. It seemed to strike a chord among the disembodied living on the Net. People copied it and sent it to one another. Over the next several months I received almost a megabyte of electronic mail from all over the planet, mostly from folks whose faces I have never seen and probably never will.

They told me of their own tragedies and what they had done to 41 survive them. As humans have since words were first uttered, we shared the second most common human experience, death, with an openheartedness that would have caused grave uneasiness in physical America, where the whole topic is so cloaked in denial as to be considered obscene. Those strangers, who had no arms to put around my shoulders, no eyes to weep with mine, nevertheless saw me through. As neighbors do.

I have no idea how far we will plunge into this strange place. 42 Unlike previous frontiers, this one has no end. It is so dissatisfying in so many ways that I suspect we will be more restless in our search for home here than in all our previous explorations. And that is one reason why I think we may find it after all. If home is where the heart is, then there is already some part of home to be found in cyberspace.

So . . . does virtual community work or not? Should we all go off 43 to cyberspace or should we resist it as a demonic form of symbolic abstraction? Does it supplant the real or is there, in it, reality itself?

Like so many true things, this one doesn't resolve itself to a black 44 or a white. Nor is it gray. It is, along with the rest of life, black/white. Both/neither. I'm not being equivocal or whishy-washy here. We have to get over our Manichean sense that everything is either good or bad, and the border of cyberspace seems to me a good place to leave that old set of filters.

But really it doesn't matter. We are going there whether we want 45 to or not. In five years, everyone who is reading these words will have an e-mail address, other than the determined Luddites who also eschew the telephone and electricity.

When we are all together in cyberspace we will see what the 46 human spirit, and the basic desire to connect, can create there. I am convinced that the result will be more benign if we go there open-minded, open-hearted, and excited with the adventure than if we are dragged into exile.

And we must remember that going to cyberspace, unlike previ- 47 ous great emigrations to the frontier, hardly requires us to leave where we have been. Many will find, as I have, a much richer appreciation of physical reality for having spent so much time in virtuality.

Despite its current (and perhaps in some areas permanent) insuf- 48 ficiencies, we should go to cyberspace with hope. Groundless hope, like unconditional love, may be the only kind that counts.

5

LANGUAGE

SEX, LIES, AND CONVERSATION

Deborah Tannen

I was addressing a small gathering in a suburban Virginia living 1
room—a women's group that had invited men to join them.
Throughout the evening, one man had been particularly talkative,
frequently offering ideas and anecdotes, while his wife sat silently
beside him on the couch. Toward the end of the evening, I com-
mented that women frequently complain that their husbands don't
talk to them. This man quickly concurred. He gestured toward his
wife and said, "She's the talker in our family." The room burst into
laughter; the man looked puzzled and hurt. "It's true," he explained.
"When I come home from work I have nothing to say. If she didn't
keep the conversation going, we'd spend the whole evening in
silence."

This episode crystallizes the irony that although American men 2
tend to talk more than women in public situations, they often talk
less at home. And this pattern is wreaking havoc with marriage.

The pattern was observed by political scientist Andrew Hacker 3
in the late '70s. Sociologist Catherine Kohler Riessman reports in her
new book *Divorce Talk* that most of the women she interviewed—but
only a few of the men—gave lack of communication as the reason for
their divorces. Given the current divorce rate of nearly 50 percent,
that amounts to millions of cases in the United States every year—a
virtual epidemic of failed conversation.

In my own research, complaints from women about their hus- 4
bands most often focused not on tangible inequities such as having
given up the chance for a career to accompany a husband to his, or
doing far more than their share of daily life-support work like clean-

ing, cooking, social arrangements and errands. Instead, they focused on communication: "He doesn't listen to me," "He doesn't talk to me." I found, as Hacker observed years before, that most wives want their husbands to be, first and foremost, conversational partners, but few husbands share this expectation of their wives.

In short, the image that best represents the current crisis is the 5 stereotypical cartoon scene of a man sitting at the breakfast table with a newspaper held up in front of his face, while a woman glares at the back of it, wanting to talk.

Linguistic Battle of the Sexes

How can women and men have such different impressions of 6 communication in marriage? Why the widespread imbalance in their interests and expectations?

In the April issue of *American Psychologist*, Stanford University's 7 Eleanor Maccoby reports the results of her own and other's research showing that children's development is most influenced by the social structure of peer interactions. Boys and girls tend to play with children of their own gender, and their sex-separate groups have different organizational structures and interactive norms.

I believe these systematic differences in childhood socialization 8 make talk between women and men like cross-cultural communication, heir to all the attraction and pitfalls of that enticing but difficult enterprise. My research on men's and women's conversations uncovered patterns similar to those described for children's groups.

For women, as for girls, intimacy is the fabric of relationships, 9 and talk is the thread from which it is woven. Little girls create and maintain friendships by exchanging secrets; similarly, women regard conversation as the cornerstone of friendship. So a woman expects her husband to be a new and improved version of a best friend. What is important is not the individual subjects that are discussed but a sense of closeness, of a life shared, that emerges when people tell their thoughts, feelings, and impressions.

Bonds between boys can be as intense as girls', but they are 10 based less on talking, more on doing things together. Since they don't assume talk is the cement that binds a relationship, men don't know what kind of talk women want and they don't miss it when it isn't there.

Boys' groups are larger, more inclusive, and more hierarchical, so 11 boys must struggle to avoid the subordinate position in the group.

This may play a role in women's complaints that men don't listen to them. Some men really don't like to listen, because being the listener makes them feel one-down, like a child listening to adults or an employee to a boss.

But often when women tell men, "You aren't listening," and the 12 men protest, "I am," the men are right. The impression of not listening results from misalignments in the mechanics of conversation. The misalignment begins as soon as a man and a woman take physical positions. This became clear when I studied videotapes made by psychologist Bruce Dorval of children and adults talking to their same-sex best friends. I found that at every age, the girls and women faced each other directly, their eyes anchored on each other's faces. At every age, the boys and men sat at angles to each other and looked elsewhere in the room, periodically glancing at each other. They were obviously attuned to each other, often mirroring each other's movements. But the tendency of men to face away can give women the impression they aren't listening even when they are. A young woman in college was frustrated: Whenever she told her boyfriend she wanted to talk to him, he would lie down on the floor, close his eyes, and put his arm over his face. This signaled to her, "He's taking a nap." But he insisted he was listening extra hard. Normally, he looks around the room, so he is easily distracted. Lying down and covering his eyes helped him concentrate on what she was saying.

Analogous to the physical alignment that women and men take 13 in conversation is their topical alignment. The girls in my study tended to talk at length about one topic, but the boys tended to jump from topic to topic. The second-grade girls exchanged stories about people they knew. The second-grade boys teased, told jokes, noticed things in the room and talked about finding games to play. The sixth-grade girls talked about problems with a mutual friend. The sixth-grade boys talked about 55 different topics, none of which extended over more than a few turns.

Listening to Body Language

Switching topics is another habit that gives women the impres- 14 sion men aren't listening, especially if they switch to a topic about themselves. But the evidence of the tenth-grade boys in my study indicates otherwise. The tenth-grade boys sprawled across their chairs with bodies parallel and eyes straight ahead, rarely looking at each other. They looked as if they were riding in a car, staring out the windshield. But they were talking about their feelings. One boy was upset because a girl had told him he had a drinking problem, and the other was feeling alienated from all his friends.

Now, when a girl told a friend about a problem, the friend 15 responded by asking probing questions and expressing agreement and understanding. But the boys dismissed each other's problems. Todd assured Richard that his drinking was "no big problem" because "sometimes you're funny when you're off your butt." And when Todd said he felt left out, Richard responded, "Why should you? You know more people than me."

Women perceive such responses as belittling and unsupportive. 16 But the boys seemed satisfied with them. Whereas women reassure each other by implying, "You shouldn't feel bad because I've had similar experiences," men do so by implying, "You shouldn't feel bad because your problems aren't so bad."

There are even simpler reasons for women's impression that men 17 don't listen. Linguist Lynette Hirschman found that women make more listener-noise, such as "mhm," "uhuh," and "yeah," to show "I'm with you." Men, she found, more often give silent attention. Women who expect a stream of listener-noise interpret silent attention as no attention at all.

Women's conversational habits are as frustrating to men as men's 18 are to women. Men who expect silent attention interpret a stream of listener-noise as overreaction or impatience. Also, when women talk to each other in a close, comfortable setting, they often overlap, finish each other's sentences and anticipate what the other is about to say. This practice, which I call "participatory listenership," is often perceived by men as interruption, intrusion and lack of attention.

A parallel difference caused a man to complain about his wife, 19 "She just wants to talk about her own point of view. If I show her another view, she gets mad at me." When most women talk to each other, they assume a conversationalist's job is to express agreement and support. But many men see their conversational duty as pointing out the other side of an argument. This is heard as disloyalty by women, and refusal to offer the requisite support. It is not that women don't want to see other points of view, but that they prefer them phrased as suggestions and inquiries rather than as direct challenges.

In his book *Fighting for Life*, Walter Ong points out that men use 20 "agonistic" or warlike, oppositional formats to do almost anything; thus discussion becomes debate, and conversation a competitive sport. In contrast, women see conversation as a ritual means of establishing rapport. If Jane tells a problem and June says she has a similar one, they walk away feeling closer to each other. But this attempt at establishing rapport can backfire when used with men. Men take too literally women's ritual "troubles talk," just as women mistake men's ritual challenges for real attack.

The Sounds of Silence

These differences begin to clarify why women and men have [21] such different expectations about communication in marriage. For women, talk creates intimacy. Marriage is an orgy of closeness: you can tell your feelings and thoughts, and still be loved. Their greatest fear is being pushed away. But men live in a hierarchical world, where talk maintains independence and status. They are on guard to protect themselves from being put down and pushed around.

This explains the paradox of the talkative man who said of his [22] silent wife, "She's the talker." In the public setting of a guest lecture, he felt challenged to show his intelligence and display his understanding of the lecture. But at home, where he has nothing to prove and no one to defend against, he is free to remain silent. For his wife, being home means she is free from the worry that something she says might offend someone, or spark disagreement, or appear to be showing off; at home she is free to talk.

The communication problems that endanger marriage can't be [23] fixed by mechanical engineering. They require a new conceptual framework about the role of talk in human relationships. Many of the psychological explanations that have become second nature may not be helpful, because they tend to blame either women (for not being assertive enough) or men (for not being in touch with their feelings). A sociolinguistic approach by which male-female conversation is seen as cross-cultural communication allows us to understand the problem and forge solutions without blaming either party.

Once the problem is understood, improvement comes naturally, [24] as it did to the young woman and her boyfriend who seemed to go to sleep when she wanted to talk. Previously, she had accused him of not listening, and he had refused to change his behavior, since that would be admitting fault. But then she learned about and explained to him the differences in women's and men's habitual ways of aligning themselves in conversation. The next time she told him she wanted to talk, he began, as usual, by lying down and covering his eyes. When the familiar negative reaction bubbled up, she reassured herself that he really was listening. But then he sat up and looked at her. Thrilled, she asked why. He said, "You like me to look at you when we talk, so I'll try to do it." Once he saw their differences as cross-cultural rather than right and wrong, he independently altered his behavior.

Women who feel abandoned and deprived when their husbands 25 won't listen to or report daily news may be happy to discover their husbands trying to adapt once they understand the place of small talk in women's relationships. But if their husbands don't adapt, the women may still be comforted that for men, this is not a failure of intimacy. Accepting the difference, the wives may look to their friends or family for that kind of talk. And husbands who can't provide it shouldn't feel their wives have made unreasonable demands. Some couples will still decide to divorce, but at least their decisions will be based on realistic expectations.

In these times of resurgent ethnic conflicts, the world desperately 26 needs cross-cultural understanding. Like charity, successful cross-cultural communication should begin at home.

ARIA[1]

Richard Rodriguez

Supporters of bilingual education today imply that students like me miss a great deal by not being taught in their family's language. What they seem not to recognize is that, as a socially disadvantaged child,. I considered Spanish to be a private language. What I needed to learn in school was that I had the right—and the obligation—to speak the public language of *los gringos*.[2] The odd truth is that my first-grade classmates could have become bilingual, in the conventional sense of that word, more easily than I. Had they been taught (as upper-middle-class children are often taught early) a second language like Spanish or French, they could have regarded it simply as that: another public language. In my case such bilingualism could not have been so quickly achieved. What I did not believe was that I could speak a single public language.

Without question, it would have pleased me to hear my teachers address me in Spanish when I entered the classroom. I would have felt much less afraid. I would have trusted them and responded with ease. But I would have delayed—for how long postponed?—having to learn the language of public society, I would have evaded—and for how long could I have afforded to delay?—learning the great lesson of school, that I had a public identity.

Fortunately, my teachers were unsentimental about their responsibility. What they understood was that I needed to speak a public language. So their voices would search me out, asking me questions. Each time I'd hear them, I'd look up in surprise to see a nun's face frowning at me. I'd mumble, not really meaning to answer. The nun would persist, "Richard, stand up. Don't look at the floor. Speak up. Speak to the entire class, not just to me!" But I couldn't believe that the English language was mine to use. (In part, I did not want to believe it.) I continued to mumble. I resisted the teacher's demands. (Did I somehow suspect that once I learned public language my pleasing family life would be changed?) Silent, waiting for the bell to sound, I remained dazed, diffident, afraid.

Because I wrongly imagined that English was intrinsically a public language and Spanish an intrinsically private one, I easily noted the difference between classroom language and the language of

---

[1] Solo vocal piece with instrumental accompaniment or melody.
[2] Foreigners, especially Americans.

home. At school, words were directed to a general audience of listeners. ("Boys and girls.") Words were meaningfully ordered. And the point was not self-expression alone but to make oneself understood by many others. The teacher quizzed: "Boys and girls, why do we use that word in this sentence? Could we think of a better word to use there? Would the sentence change its meaning if the words were differently arranged? And wasn't there a better way of saying much the same thing?" (I couldn't say. I wouldn't try to say.)

Three months. Five. Half a year passed. Unsmiling, ever watch-   5
ful, my teachers noted my silence. They began to connect my behavior with the difficult progress my older sister and brother were making. Until one Saturday morning three nuns arrived at the house to talk to our parents. Stiffly, they sat on the blue living room sofa. From the doorway of another room, spying the visitors, I noted the incongruity—the clash of two worlds, the faces and voices of school intruding upon the familiar setting of home. I overheard one voice gently wondering, "Do your children speak only Spanish at home, Mrs. Rodriguez?" While another voice added, "That Richard especially seems so timid and shy."

That Rich-heard!   6

With great tact the visitors continued, "Is it possible for you and   7
your husband to encourage your children to practice their English when they are home?" Of course, my parents complied. What would they not do for their children's well-being? And how could they have questioned the Church's authority which those women represented? In an instant, they agreed to give up the language (the sounds) that had revealed and accentuated our family's closeness. The moment after the visitors left, the change was observed, "*Ahora*, speak to us *en inglés*,[3] my father and mother united to tell us.

At first, it seemed a kind of game. After dinner each night, the   8
family gathered to practice "our" English. (It was still then *inglés*, a language foreign to us, so we felt drawn as strangers to it.) Laughing, we would try to define words we could not pronounce. We played with strange English sounds, often overanglicizing our pronunciations. And we filled the smiling gaps of our sentences with familiar Spanish sounds. But that was cheating, somebody shouted. Everyone laughed. In school, meanwhile, like my brother and sister, I was required to attend a daily tutoring session. I needed a full year of special attention. I also needed my teachers to keep my attention from straying in class by calling out, *Rich-heard*—their English voices

---

[3] "Now, speak to us in English."

slowly prying loose my ties to my other name, its three notes, *Ri-car-do*. Most of all I needed to hear my mother and father speak to me in a moment of seriousness in broken—suddenly heartbreaking—English. The scene was inevitable: One Saturday morning I entered the kitchen where my parents were talking in Spanish. I did not realize that they were talking in Spanish however until, at the moment they saw me, I heard their voices change to speak English. Those *gringo* sounds they uttered startled me. Pushed me away. In that moment of trivial misunderstanding and profound insight, I felt my throat twisted by unsounded grief. I turned away quickly and left the room. But I had no place to escape to with Spanish. (The spell was broken.) My brother and sisters were speaking English in another part of the house.

Again and again in the days following, increasingly angry, I was 9 obliged to hear my mother and father: "Speak to us *en inglés*" (*Speak.*) Only then did I determine to learn classroom English. Weeks after, it happened: One day in school I raised my hand to volunteer an answer. I spoke out in a loud voice. And I did not think it remarkable when the entire class understood. That day, I moved very far from the disadvantaged child I had been only days earlier. The belief, that calming assurance that I belonged in public, had at last taken hold.

Shortly after, I stopped hearing the high and loud sounds of *los* 10 *gringos*. A more and more confident speaker of English, I didn't trouble to listen to *how* strangers sounded, speaking to me. And there simply were too many English-speaking people in my day for me to hear American accents anymore. Conversations quickened. Listening to persons who sounded eccentrically pitched voices, I usually noted their sounds for an initial few seconds before I concentrated on *what* they were saying. Conversations became content-full. Transparent. Hearing someone's *tone* of voice—angry or questioning or sarcastic or happy or sad—I didn't distinguish it from the words it expressed. Sound and word were thus tightly wedded. At the end of a day, I was often bemused, always relieved, to realized how "silent," though crowded with words, my day in public had been. (This public silence measured and quickened the change in my life.)

At last, seven years old, I came to believe what had been techni- 11 cally true since my birth; I was an American citizen.

But the special feeling of closeness at home was diminished by 12 then. Gone was the desperate, urgent, intense feeling of being at home, rare was the experience of feeling myself individualized by family intimates. We remained a loving family, but one greatly changed. No longer so close; no longer bound tight by the pleasing and troubling knowledge of our public separateness. Neither my older brother nor sister rushed home after school anymore. Nor did I. When I arrived home there would often be neighborhood kids in the house. Or the house would be empty of sounds.

Following the dramatic Americanization of their children, even my parents grew more publicly confident. Especially my mother. She learned the names of all the people on our block. And she decided we needed to have a telephone installed in the house. My father continued to use the word *gringo*. But it was no longer charged with the old bitterness of distrust. (Stripped of any emotional content, the word simply became a name for those Americans not of Hispanic descent.) Hearing him, sometimes, I wasn't sure if he was pronouncing the Spanish word *gringo* or saying gringo in English. 13

Matching the silence I started hearing in public was a new quiet at home. The family's quiet was partly due to the fact that, as we children learned more and more English, we shared fewer and fewer words with our parents. Sentences needed to be spoken slowly when a child addressed his mother or father. (Often the parent wouldn't understand.) The child would need to repeat himself. (Still the parent misunderstood.) The young voice, frustrated, would end up saying, "Never mind"—the subject was closed. Dinners would be noisy with the clinking of knives and forks against dishes. My mother would smile softly between her remarks; my father at the other end of the table would chew and chew at his food, while he stared over the heads of his children. 14

My *mother!* My *father!* After English became my primary language, I no longer knew what words to use in addressing my parents. The old Spanish words (those tender accents of sound) I had used earlier—*mamá* and *papá*—I couldn't use anymore. They would have been too painful reminders of how much had changed in my life. On the other hand, the words I heard neighborhood kids call their parents seemed equally unsatisfactory. *Mother* and *Father; Ma, Papa, Pa, Dad, Pop* (how I hated the all American sound of that last word especially)—all these terms I felt were unsuitable, not really terms of address for my parents. As a result, I never used them at home. Whenever I'd speak to my parents, I would try to get their attention with eye contact alone. In public conversations, I'd refer to "my parents" or "my mother and father." 15

My mother and father, for their part, responded differently, as their children spoke to them less. She grew restless, seemed troubled and anxious at the scarcity of words exchanged in the house. It was she who would question me about my day when I came home from 16 school. She smiled at small talk. She pried at the edges of my sentences to get me to say something more. (What?) She'd join conversations she overheard, but her intrusions often stopped her children's talking. By contrast, my father seemed reconciled to the new quiet. Though his English improved somewhat, he retired into silence. At dinner he spoke very little. One night his children and even his wife helplessly giggled at his garbled English pronunciation of the Catholic Grace before Meals. Thereafter he made his wife recite the prayer at the start of each meal, even on formal occasions, when there were guests in the house. Hers became the public voice of the family. On official business, it was she, not my father, one would usually hear on the phone or in stores, talking to strangers. His children grew so accustomed to his silence that, years later, they would speak routinely of his shyness. (My mother would often try to explain: Both his parents died when he was eight. He was raised by an uncle who treated him like little more than a menial servant. He was never encouraged to speak. He grew up alone. A man of few words.) But my father was not shy, I realized, when I'd watch him speaking Spanish with relatives. Using Spanish, he was quickly effusive. Especially when talking with other men, his voice would spark, flicker, flare alive with sounds. In Spanish, he expressed ideas and feelings he rarely revealed in English. With firm Spanish sounds, he conveyed confidence and authority English would never allow him.

The silence at home, however, was finally more than a literal 17 silence. Fewer words passed between parent and child, but more profound was the silence that resulted from my inattention to sounds. At about the time I no longer bothered to listen with care to the sounds of English in public, I grew careless about listening to the sounds family members made when they spoke. Most of the time I heard someone speaking at home and didn't distinguish his sounds from the words people uttered in public. I didn't even pay much attention to my parents' accented and ungrammatical speech. At least not at home. Only when I was with them in public would I grow alert to their accents. Though, even then, their sounds caused me less and less concern. For I was increasingly confident of my own public identity.

I would have been happier about my public success had I not 18 sometimes recalled what it had been like earlier, when my family had conveyed its intimacy through a set of conveniently private sounds. Sometimes in public, hearing a stranger, I'd hark back to my past. A Mexican farmworker approached me downtown to ask directions to somewhere, "*¿Hijito. . . ?*"[4] he said. And his voice summoned deep

---

[4] "Little boy. . . ?"

longing. Another time, standing beside my mother in the visiting room of a Carmelite convent, before the dense screen which rendered the nuns shadowy figures, I heard several Spanish-speaking nuns—their busy, singsong overlapping voices—assure us that yes, yes, we were remembered, all our family was remembered in their prayers. (Their voices echoed faraway family sounds.) Another day, a dark-faced old woman—her hand light on my shoulder—steadied herself against me as she boarded a bus. She murmured something I couldn't quite comprehend. Her Spanish voice came near, like the face of a never-before-seen relative in the instant before I was kissed. Her voice, like so many of the Spanish voices I'd hear in public, recalled the golden age of my youth. Hearing Spanish then, I continued to be a careful, if sad, listener to sounds. Hearing a Spanish-speaking family walking behind me, I turned to look. I smiled for an instant, before my glance found the Hispanic-looking faces of strangers in the crowd going by.

Today I hear bilingual educators say that children lose a degree of 19 "individuality" by becoming assimilated into public society. (Bilingual schooling was popularized in the seventies, that decade when middle-class ethnics began to resist the process of assimilation—the American melting pot). But the bilingualists simplistically scorn the value and necessity of assimilation. They do not seem to realize that there are *two* ways a person is individualized. So they do not realize that while one suffers a diminished sense of *private* individuality by becoming assimilated into public society, such assimilation makes possible the achievement of *public* individuality.

The bilingualists insist that a student should be reminded of 20 his difference from others in mass society, his heritage. But they equate mere separateness with individuality. The fact is that only in private—with intimates—is separateness from the crowd a prerequisite for individuality. (An intimate draws me apart, tells me that I am unique, unlike all others.) In public, by contrast, full individuality is achieved, paradoxically, by those who are able to consider themselves members of the crowd. Thus it happened for me: Only when I was able to think of myself as an American, no longer an alien in *gringo* society, could I seek the rights and opportunities necessary for full public individuality. The social and political advantages I enjoy as a man result from the day that I came to believe that my name, indeed, is *Rich-heard Road-ree-guess*. It is true that my public society today is often impersonal. (My public society is usually mass society). Yet despite the anonymity of the crowd and despite the fact that the individuality I achieve in public is often tenuous—because it depends on my being one in a crowd—I celebrate the day I acquired my new name. Those middle-class ethnics who scorn assimilation seem to me filled with decadent self-pity, obsessed by the burden of public life. Dangerously, they romanticize public separateness and they trivialize the dilemma of the socially disadvantaged.

My awkward childhood does not prove the necessity of bilingual education. My story discloses instead an essential myth of childhood—inevitable pain. If I rehearse here the changes in my private life after my Americanization, it is finally to emphasize the public gain. The loss implies the gain: The house I returned to each afternoon was quiet. Intimate sounds no longer rushed to the door to greet me. There were other noises inside. The telephone rang. Neighborhood kids ran past the door of the bedroom where I was reading my schoolbooks—covered with shopping-bag paper. Once I learned public language, it would never again be easy for me to hear intimate family voices. More and more of my day was spent hearing words. But that may only be a way of saying that the day I raised my hand in class and spoke loudly to an entire roomful of faces, my childhood started to end.

The Day Language Came into My Life

Helen Keller

The most important day I remember in all my life is the one on 1
which my teacher, Anne Mansfield Sullivan, came to me. I am filled
with wonder when I consider the immeasurable contrast between the
two lives which it connects. It was the third of March 1887, three
months before I was seven years old.

On the afternoon of that eventful day, I stood on the porch, 2
dumb, expectant. I guessed vaguely from my mother's signs and
from the hurrying to and fro in the house that something unusual
was about to happen, so I went to the door and waited on the steps.
The afternoon sun penetrated the mass of honeysuckle that covered
the porch and fell on my upturned face. My fingers lingered almost
unconsciously on the familiar leaves and blossoms which had just
come forth to greet the sweet southern spring. I did not know what
the future held of marvel or surprise for me. Anger and bitterness
had preyed upon me continually for weeks and a deep languor had
succeeded this passionate struggle.

Have you ever been at sea in a dense fog, when it seemed as if a 3
tangible white darkness shut you in, and the great ship, tense and
anxious, groped her way toward the shore with plummet and sounding-line, and you waited with beating heart for something to happen? I was like that ship before my education began, only I was
without compass or sounding-line and had no way of knowing how
near the harbor was. "Light! give me light!" was the wordless cry of
my soul, and the light of love shone on me in that very hour.

I felt approaching footsteps. I stretched out my hand as I sup- 4
posed to my mother. Someone took it, and I was caught up and held
close in the arms of her who had come to reveal all things to me, and,
more than all things else, to love me.

The morning after my teacher came she led me into her room 5
and gave me a doll. The little blind children at the Perkins Institution
had sent it and Laura Bridgman had dressed it; but I did not know
this until afterward. When I had played with it a little while, Miss
Sullivan slowly spelled into my hand the word "d-o-l-l." I was at
once interested in this finger play and tried to imitate it. When I
finally succeeded in making the letters correctly I was flushed with
childish pleasure and pride. Running downstairs to my mother I held

up my hand and made the letters for doll. I did not know that I was spelling a word or even that words existed; I was simply making my fingers go in monkeylike imitation. In the days that followed I learned to spell in this uncomprehending way a great many words, among them *pin, hat, cup* and a few verbs like *sit, stand* and *walk.* But my teacher had been with me several weeks before I understood that everything has a name.

One day, while I was playing with my new doll, Miss Sullivan put 6 my big rag doll into my lap also, spelled "d-o-l-l" and tried to make me understand that "d-o-l-l" applied to both. Earlier in the day we had had a tussle over the words "m-u-g" and "w-a-t-e-r." Miss Sullivan had tried to impress it upon me that "m-u-g" is *mug* and that "w-a-t-e-r" is *water,* but I persisted in confounding the two. In despair she had dropped the subject for the time, only to renew it at the first opportunity. I became impatient at her repeated attempts and, seizing the new doll, I dashed it upon the floor. I was keenly delighted when I felt the fragments of the broken doll at my feet. Neither sorrow nor regret followed my passionate outburst. I had not loved the doll. In the still, dark world in which I lived there was no strong sentiment or tenderness. I felt my teacher sweep the fragments to one side of the hearth, and I had a sense of satisfaction that the cause of my discomfort was removed. She brought me my hat, and I knew I was going out into the warm sunshine. This thought, if a wordless sensation may be called a thought, made me hop and skip with pleasure.

We walked down the path to the well-house, attracted by the fra- 7 grance of the honeysuckle with which it was covered. Some one was drawing water and my teacher placed my hand under the spout. As the cool stream gushed over one hand she spelled into the other the word *water,* first slowly, then rapidly. I stood still, my whole attention fixed upon the motions of her fingers. Suddenly I felt a misty consciousness as of something forgotten—a thrill of returning thought; and somehow the mystery of language was revealed to me. I knew then that "w-a-t-e-r" meant the wonderful cool something that was flowing over my hand. The living word awakened my soul, gave it light, hope, joy, set it free! There were barriers still, it is true, but barriers that could in time be swept away.

I left the well-house eager to learn. Everything had a name, and 8 each name gave birth to a new thought. As we returned to the house every object which I touched seemed to quiver with life. That was because I saw everything with the strange, new sight that had come to me. On entering the door I remembered the doll I had broken. I felt my way to the hearth and picked up the pieces. I tried vainly to put them together. Then my eyes filled with tears; for I realized what I had done, and for the first time I felt repentance and sorrow.

I learned a great many new words that day. I do not remember 9 what they all were; but I do know that *mother, father, sister, teacher* were among them—words that were to make the world blossom for me, "like Aaron's rod, with flowers." It would have been difficult to find a happier child than I was as I lay in my crib at the close of that eventful day and lived over the joys it had brought me, and for the first time longed for a new day to come.

6

ADVERTISEMENTS

THE COOLHUNT

Malcolm Gladwell

Who decides what's cool? Certain kids in certain places—and only the coolhunters know who they are.

1.

Baysie Wightman met DeeDee Gordon, appropriately enough, on a coolhunt. It was 1992. Baysie was a big shot for Converse, and DeeDee, who was barely twenty-one, was running a very cool boutique called Placid Planet, on Newbury Street in Boston. Baysie came in with a camera crew—one she often used when she was coolhunting—and said, "I've been watching your store, I've seen you, I've heard you know what's up," because it was Baysie's job at Converse to find people who knew what was up and she thought DeeDee was one of those people. DeeDee says that she responded with reserve—that "I was like, 'Whatever.'"—but Baysie said that if DeeDee ever wanted to come and work at Converse she should just call, and nine months later DeeDee called. This was about the time the cool kids had decided they didn't want the hundred-and-twenty-five-dollar basketball sneaker with seventeen different kinds of high-technology materials and colors and air-cushioned heels anymore. They wanted simplicity and authenticity, and Baysie picked up on that. She brought back the Converse One Star, which was a vulcanized, suede, low-top classic old-school sneaker from the nineteen-seventies, and, sure enough, the One Star quickly became the signature shoe of the retro era. Remember what Kurt Cobain was wearing in the famous picture of him lying dead on the ground after committing suicide? Black Converse One Stars. DeeDee's big score was calling the sandal craze. She had been out in Los Angeles and had kept seeing the white teen-age girls dressing up like cholos, Mexican gangsters, in tight white tank tops known as "wife beaters," with a bra strap hanging out, and long shorts and tube socks and shower sandals. DeeDee recalls, "I'm like, 'I'm telling you, Baysie, this is going to hit. There are just too many people wearing it. We have to make a shower sandal.'" So Baysie, DeeDee, and a designer came up with the idea of making a retro sneaker-sandal, cutting the back off the One Star and putting a thick outsole on it. It was huge, and, amazingly, it's still huge.

Today, Baysie works for Reebok as general-merchandise 2 manager—part of the team trying to return Reebok to the position it enjoyed in the mid-nineteen-eighties as the country's hottest sneaker company. DeeDee works for an advertising agency in Del Mar called Lambesis, where she puts out a quarterly tip sheet called the L Report on what the cool kids in major American cities are thinking and doing and buying. Baysie and DeeDee are best friends. They talk on the phone all the time.

They get together whenever Baysie is in L.A. (DeeDee: "It's, like, 3 how many times can you drive past O.J. Simpson's house?"), and between them they can talk for hours about the art of the coolhunt. They're the Lewis and Clark of cool.

What they have is what everybody seems to want these days, 4 which is a window on the world of the street. Once, when fashion trends were set by the big couture houses—when cool was trickle-down—that wasn't important. But sometime in the past few decades things got turned over, and fashion became trickle-up. It's now about chase and flight—designers and retailers and the mass consumer giving chase to the elusive prey of street cool—and the rise of coolhunting as a profession shows how serious the chase has become. The sneakers of Nike and Reebok used to come out yearly. Now a new style comes out every season. Apparel designers used to have an eighteen-month lead time between concept and sale. Now they're reducing that to a year, or even six months, in order to react faster to new ideas from the street. The paradox, of course, is that the better coolhunters become at bringing the mainstream close to the cutting edge, the more elusive the cutting edge becomes. This is the first rule of the cool: The quicker the chase, the quicker the flight. The act of discovering what's cool is what causes cool to move on, which explains the triumphant circularity of coolhunting: because we have coolhunters like DeeDee and Baysie, cool changes more quickly, and because cool changes more quickly, we need coolhunters like DeeDee and Baysie.

DeeDee is tall and glamorous, with short hair she has dyed so often that she claims to have forgotten her real color. She drives a yellow 1977 Trans Am with a burgundy stripe down the center and a 1973 Mercedes 450 SL, and lives in a spare, Japanese-style cabin in Laurel Canyon. She uses words like "rad" and "totally," and offers non-stop, deadpan pronouncements on pop culture, as in "It's all about Pee-wee Herman." She sounds at first like a teen, like the same teens who, at Lambesis, it is her job to follow. But teen speech—particularly girl-teen speech, with its fixation on reported speech ("so she goes," "and I'm like," "and he goes") and its stock vocabulary of accompanying grimaces and gestures—is about using language less to communicate than to fit in. DeeDee uses teen speech to set herself apart, and the result is, for lack of a better word, really cool. She doesn't do the teen thing of climbing half an octave at the end of every sentence. Instead, she drags out her vowels for emphasis, so that if she mildly disagreed with something I'd said she would say "Maalcolm" and if she strongly disagreed with what I'd said she would say "Maaalcolm."

Baysie is older, just past forty (although you would never guess that), and went to Exeter and Middlebury and had two grandfathers who went to Harvard (although you wouldn't guess that, either). She has curly brown hair and big green eyes and long legs and so much energy that it is hard to imagine her asleep, or resting, or even standing still for longer than thirty seconds. The hunt for cool is an obsession with her, and DeeDee is the same way. DeeDee used to sit on the corner of West Broadway and Prince in SoHo—back when SoHo was cool—and take pictures of everyone who walked by for an entire hour. Baysie can tell you precisely where she goes on her Reebok coolhunts to find the really cool alternative white kids ("I'd maybe go to Portland and hang out where the skateboarders hang out near that bridge") or which snowboarding mountain has cooler kids—Stratton, in Vermont, or Summit County, in Colorado. (Summit, definitely.) DeeDee can tell you on the basis of the L Report's research exactly how far Dallas is behind New York in coolness (from six to eight months). Baysie is convinced that Los Angeles is not happening right now: "In the early nineteen-nineties a lot more was coming from L.A. They had a big trend with the whole Melrose Avenue look—the stupid goatees, the shorter hair. It was cleaned-up after-grunge. There were a lot of places you could go to buy vinyl records. It was a strong place to go for looks. Then it went back to being horrible." DeeDee is convinced that Japan is happening: "I linked onto this future-technology thing two years ago. Now look at it, it's huge. It's the whole resurgence of Nike—Nike being larger than life. I went to Japan and saw the kids just bailing the most technologically advanced Nikes with their little dresses and little outfits and I'm like, 'Whoa, this is trippy!' It's performance mixed with fashion. It's really superheavy." Baysie has a theory that Liverpool is cool right now because it's the birthplace of the whole "lad" look, which involves soccer blokes in the pubs going superdressy and wearing Dolce & Gabbana and Polo Sport and Reebok Classics on their feet. But when I asked DeeDee about that, she just rolled her eyes: "Sometimes Baysie goes off on these tangents. Man, I love that woman!"

I used to think that if I talked to Baysie and DeeDee long enough 7 I could write a coolhunting manual, an encyclopedia of cool. But then I realized that the manual would have so many footnotes and caveats that it would be unreadable. Coolhunting is not about the articulation of a coherent philosophy of cool. It's just a collection of spontaneous observations and predictions that differ from one moment to the next and from one coolhunter to the next. Ask a coolhunter where the baggy-jeans look came from, for example, and you might get any number of answers: urban black kids mimicking the jailhouse look, skateboarders looking for room to move, snowboarders trying not to look like skiers, or, alternatively, all three at once, in some grand concordance.

Or take the question of exactly how Tommy Hilfiger—a forty- 8 five-year-old white guy from Greenwich, Connecticut, doing all-American preppy clothes—came to be the designer of choice for urban black America. Some say it was all about the early and visible endorsement given Hilfiger by the hip-hop auteur Grand Puba, who wore a dark-green-and-blue Tommy jacket over a white Tommy T-shirt as he leaned on his black Lamborghini on the cover of the hugely influential "Grand Puba 2000" CD, and whose love for Hilfiger soon spread to other rappers. (Who could forget the rhymes of Mobb Deep? "Tommy was my nigga / And couldn't figure / How me and Hilfiger / used to move through with vigor.") Then I had lunch with one of Hilfiger's designers, a twenty-six-year-old named Ulrich (Ubi) Simpson, who has a Puerto Rican mother and a Dutch-Venezuelan father, plays lacrosse, snowboards, surfs the long board, goes to hip-hop concerts, listens to Jungle, Edith Piaf, opera, rap, and Metallica, and has working with him on his design team a twenty-seven-year-old black guy from Montclair with dreadlocks, a twenty-two-year-old Asian-American who lives on the Lower East Side, a twenty-five-year-old South Asian guy from Fiji, and a twenty-one-year-old white graffiti artist from Queens. That's when it occurred to me that maybe the reason Tommy Hilfiger can make white culture cool to black culture is that he has people working for him who are cool in both cultures simultaneously. Then again, maybe it was all Grand Puba. Who knows?

One day last month, Baysie took me on a coolhunt to the Bronx 9 and Harlem, lugging a big black canvas bag with twenty-four different shoes that Reebok is about to bring out, and as we drove down Fordham Road, she had her head out the window like a little kid, checking out what everyone on the street was wearing. We went to Dr. Jay's, which is the cool place to buy sneakers in the Bronx, and Baysie crouched down on the floor and started pulling the shoes out of her bag one by one, soliciting opinions from customers who gathered around and asking one question after another, in rapid sequence. One guy she listened closely to was maybe eighteen or nineteen, with a diamond stud in his ear and a thin beard. He was wearing a Polo baseball cap, a brown leather jacket, and the big, oversized leather boots that are everywhere uptown right now. Baysie would hand him a shoe and he would hold it, look at the top, and move it up and down and flip it over. The first one he didn't like: "Oh-kay." The second one he hated: he made a growling sound in his throat even before Baysie could give it to him, as if to say, "Put it back in the bag—now!" But when she handed him a new DMX RXT—a low-cut run/walk shoe in white and blue and mesh with a translucent "ice" sole, which retails for a hundred and ten dollars—he looked at it long and hard and shook his head in pure admiration and just said two words, dragging each of them out: "No doubt."

Baysie was interested in what he was saying, because the DMX 10 RXT she had was a girls' shoe that actually hadn't been doing all that well. Later, she explained to me that the fact that the boys loved the shoe was critical news, because it suggested that Reebok had a potential hit if it just switched the shoe to the men's section. How she managed to distill this piece of information from the crowd of teenagers around her, how she made any sense of the two dozen shoes in her bag, most of which (to my eyes, anyway) looked pretty much the same, and how she knew which of the teens to really focus on was a mystery. Baysie is a Wasp from New England, and she crouched on the floor in Dr. Jay's for almost an hour, talking and joking with the homeboys without a trace of condescension or self-consciousness.

Near the end of her visit, a young boy walked up and sat down 11 on the bench next to her. He was wearing a black woolen cap with white stripes pulled low, a blue North Face pleated down jacket, a pair of baggy Guess jeans, and, on his feet, Nike Air Jordans. He couldn't have been more than thirteen. But when he started talking you could see Baysie's eyes light up, because somehow she knew the kid was the real thing.

"How many pairs of shoes do you buy a month?" Baysie asked. [12]

"Two," the kid answered. "And if at the end I find one more I like [13] I get to buy that, too."

Baysie was onto him. "Does your mother spoil you?" [14]

The kid blushed, but a friend next to him was laughing. [15] "Whatever he wants, he gets."

Baysie laughed, too. She had the DMX RXT in his size. He tried [16] them on. He rocked back and forth, testing them. He looked back at Baysie. He was dead serious now: "Make sure these come out."

Baysie handed him the new "Rush" Emmitt Smith shoe due out [17] in the fall. One of the boys had already pronounced it "phat," and another had looked through the marbleized-foam cradle in the heel and cried out in delight, "This is bug!" But this kid was the acid test, because this kid knew cool. He paused. He looked at it hard. "Reebok," he said, soberly and carefully, "is trying to get butter."

In the car on the way back to Manhattan, Baysie repeated it [18] twice. "Not better. Butter! That kid could totally tell you what he thinks." Baysie had spent an hour coolhunting in a shoe store and found out that Reebok's efforts were winning the highest of hip-hop praise. "He was so fucking smart."

2.

If you want to understand how trends work, and why coolhunters [19] like Baysie and DeeDee have become so important, a good place to start is with what's known as diffusion research, which is the study of how ideas and innovations spread. Diffusion researchers do things like spending five years studying the adoption of irrigation techniques in a Colombian mountain village, or developing complex matrices to map the spread of new math in the Pittsburgh school system. What they do may seem like a far cry from, say, how the Tommy Hilfiger thing spread from Harlem to every suburban mall in the country, but it really isn't: both are about how new ideas spread from one person to the next.

One of the most famous diffusion studies is Bruce Ryan and Neal [20] Gross's analysis of the spread of hybrid seed corn in Greene County,

Iowa, in the nineteen-thirties. The new seed corn was introduced there in about 1928, and it was superior in every respect to the seed that had been used by farmers for decades. But it wasn't adopted all at once. Of two hundred and fifty-nine farmers studied by Ryan and Gross, only a handful had started planting the new seed by 1933. In 1934, sixteen took the plunge. In 1935, twenty-one more followed; the next year, there were thirty-six, and the year after that a whopping sixty-one. The succeeding figures were then forty-six, thirty-six, four-teen, and three, until, by 1941, all but two of the two hundred and fifty-nine farmers studied were using the new seed. In the language of diffusion research, the handful of farmers who started trying hybrid seed corn at the very beginning of the thirties were the "inno-vators," the adventurous ones. The slightly larger group that fol-lowed them was the "early adopters." They were the opinion leaders in the community, the respected, thoughtful people who watched and analyzed what those wild innovators were doing and then did it themselves. Then came the big bulge of farmers in 1936, 1937, and 1938—the "early majority" and the "late majority," which is to say the deliberate and the skeptical masses, who would never try any-thing until the most respected farmers had tried it. Only after they had been converted did the "laggards," the most traditional of all, follow suit. The critical thing about this sequence is that it is almost entirely interpersonal. According to Ryan and Gross, only the inno-vators relied to any great extent on radio advertising and farm jour-nals and seed salesmen in making their decision to switch to the hybrid. Everyone else made his decision overwhelmingly because of the example and the opinions of his neighbors and peers.

Isn't this just how fashion works? A few years ago, the classic [21] brushed-suede Hush Puppies with the lightweight crepe sole—the moc-toe oxford known as the Duke and the slip-on with the golden buckle known as the Columbia—were selling barely sixty-five thou-sand pairs a year. The company was trying to walk away from the whole suede casual look entirely. It wanted to do "aspirational" shoes: "active casuals" in smooth leather, like the Mall Walker, with a Comfort Curve technology outsole and a heel stabilizer—the kind of shoes you see in Kinney's for $39.95. But then something strange started happening. Two Hush Puppies executives—Owen Baxter and Jeff Lewis—were doing a fashion shoot for their Mall Walkers and ran into a creative consultant from Manhattan named Jeffrey Miller, who informed them that the Dukes and the Columbias weren't dead, they were dead chic. "We were being told," Baxter recalls, "that there were areas in the Village, in SoHo, where the shoes were selling—in resale shops—and that people were wearing the old Hush Puppies. They were going to the ma-and-pa stores, the little stores that still carried them, and there was this authenticity of being able to say, 'I am wearing an original pair of Hush Puppies.'"

Baxter and Lewis—tall, solid, fair-haired Midwestern guys with 22 thick, shiny wedding bands—are shoe men, first and foremost. Baxter was working the cash register at his father's shoe store in Mount Prospect, Illinois, at the age of thirteen. Lewis was doing inventory in his father's shoe store in Pontiac, Michigan, at the age of seven. Baxter was in the National Guard during the 1968 Democratic Convention, in Chicago, and was stationed across the street from the Conrad Hilton downtown, right in the middle of things. Today, the two men work out of Rockford, Michigan (population thirty-eight hundred), where Hush Puppies has been making the Dukes and the Columbias in an old factory down by the Rogue River for almost forty years. They took me to the plant when I was in Rockford. In a crowded, noisy, low-slung building, factory workers stand in long rows, gluing, stapling, and sewing together shoes in dozens of bright colors, and the two executives stopped at each production station and described it in detail. Lewis and Baxter know shoes. But they would be the first to admit that they don't know cool. "Miller was saying that there is something going on with the shoes—that Isaac Mizrahi was wearing the shoes for his personal use," Lewis told me. We were seated around the conference table in the Hush Puppies headquarters in Rockford, with the snow and the trees outside and a big water tower behind us. "I think it's fair to say that at the time we had no idea who Isaac Mizrahi was."

By late 1994, things had begun to happen in a rush. First, the 23 designer John Bartlett called. He wanted to use Hush Puppies as accessories in his spring collection. Then Anna Sui called. Miller, the man from Manhattan, flew out to Michigan to give advice on a new line ("Of course, packing my own food and thinking about 'Fargo' in the corner of my mind"). A few months later, in Los Angeles, the designer Joel Fitzpatrick put a twenty-five-foot inflatable basset hound on the roof of his store on La Brea Avenue and gutted his adjoining art gallery to turn it into a Hush Puppies department, and even before he opened—while he was still painting and putting up shelves—Pee-wee Herman walked in and asked for a couple of pairs. Pee-wee Herman! "It was total word of mouth. I didn't even have a sign back then," Fitzpatrick recalls. In 1995, the company sold four hundred and thirty thousand pairs of the classic Hush Puppies. In 1996, it sold a million six hundred thousand, and that was only scratching the surface, because in Europe and the rest of the world, where Hush Puppies have a huge following—where they might out-sell the American market four to one—the revival was just beginning.

The cool kids who started wearing old Dukes and Columbias 24 from thrift shops were the innovators. Pee-wee Herman, wandering in off the street, was an early adopter. The million six hundred thousand people who bought Hush Puppies last year are the early major-ity, jumping in because the really cool people have already blazed the trail. Hush Puppies are moving through the country just the way hybrid seed corn moved through Greene County—all of which illus-trates what coolhunters can and cannot do. If Jeffrey Miller had been wrong—if cool people hadn't been digging through the thrift shops for Hush Puppies—and he had arbitrarily decided that Baxter and Lewis should try to convince non-cool people that the shoes were cool, it wouldn't have worked. You can't convince the late majority that Hush Puppies are cool, because the late majority makes its cool-ness decisions on the basis of what the early majority is doing, and you can't convince the early majority, because the early majority is looking at the early adopters, and you can't convince the early adopters, because they take their cues from the innovators. The inno-vators do get their cool ideas from people other than their peers, but the fact is that they are the last people who can be convinced by a marketing campaign that a pair of suede shoes is cool. These are, after all, the people who spent hours sifting through thrift-store bins. And why did they do that? Because their definition of cool is doing something that nobody else is doing. A company can intervene in the cool cycle. It can put its shoes on really cool celebrities and on fash-ion runways and on MTV. It can accelerate the transition from the innovator to the early adopter and on to the early majority. But it can't just manufacture cool out of thin air, and that's the second rule of cool.

At the peak of the Hush Puppies craziness last year, Hush 25 Puppies won the prize for best accessory at the Council of Fashion Designers' awards dinner, at Lincoln Center. The award was accepted by the Hush Puppies president, Louis Dubrow, who came out wearing a pair of custom-made black patent-leather Hush Puppies and stood there blinking and looking at the assembled crowd as if it were the last scene of "Close Encounters of the Third Kind." It was a strange moment. There was the president of the Hush Puppies company, of Rockford, Michigan, population thirty-eight hundred, sharing a stage with Calvin Klein and Donna Karan and Isaac Mizrahi—and all because some kids in the East Village began combing through thrift shops for old Dukes. Fashion was at the mercy of those kids, whoever they were, and it was a wonderful thing if the kids picked you, but a scary thing, too, because it meant that cool was something you could not control. You needed someone to find cool and tell you what it was.

3.

When Baysie Wightman went to Dr. Jay's, she was looking for cus- 26 tomer response to the new shoes Reebok had planned for the fourth quarter of 1997 and the first quarter of 1998. This kind of customer testing is critical at Reebok, because the last decade has not been kind to the company. In 1987, it had a third of the American athletic-shoe market, well ahead of Nike. Last year, it had sixteen per cent. "The kid in the store would say, 'I'd like this shoe if your logo wasn't on it,'" E. Scott Morris, who's a senior designer for Reebok, told me. "That's kind of a punch in the mouth. But we've all seen it. You go into a shoe store. The kid picks up the shoe and says, 'Ah, man, this is nice.' He turns the shoe around and around. He looks at it underneath. He looks at the side and he goes, 'Ah, this is Reebok,' and says, 'I ain't buying this,' and puts the shoe down and walks out. And you go, 'You was just digging it a minute ago. What happened?'" Somewhere along the way, the company lost its cool, and Reebok now faces the task not only of rebuilding its image but of making the shoes so cool that the kids in the store can't put them down.

Every few months, then, the company's coolhunters go out into 27 the field with prototypes of the upcoming shoes to find out what kids really like, and come back to recommend the necessary changes. The prototype of one recent Emmitt Smith shoe, for example, had a piece of molded rubber on the end of the tongue as a design element; it was supposed to give the shoe a certain "richness," but the kids said they thought it looked overbuilt. Then Reebok gave the shoes to the Boston College football team for wear-testing, and when they got the shoes back they found out that all the football players had cut out the rubber component with scissors. As messages go, this was hard to miss. The tongue piece wasn't cool, and on the final version of the shoe it was gone. The rule of thumb at Reebok is that if the kids in Chicago, New York, and Detroit all like a shoe, it's a guaranteed hit. More than likely, though, the coolhunt is going to turn up subtle differences from city to city, so that once the coolhunters come back the designers have to find out some way to synthesize what was heard, and pick out just those things that all the kids seemed to agree on. In New York, for example, kids in Harlem are more sophisticated and fashion-forward than kids in the Bronx, who like things a little more colorful and glitzy. Brooklyn, meanwhile, is conservative and preppy, more like Washington, D.C. For reasons no one really knows, Reeboks are coolest in Philadelphia. In Philly, in fact, the Reebok Classics are so huge they are known simply as National Anthems, as in "I'll have a pair of blue Anthems in nine and a half." Philadelphia is Reebok's innovator town. From there trends move along the East Coast, trickling all the way to Charlotte, North Carolina.

Reebok has its headquarters in Stoughton, Massachusetts, out- 28 side Boston—in a modern corporate park right off Route 24. There are basketball and tennis courts next to the building, and a health club on the ground floor that you can look directly into from the parking lot. The front lobby is adorned with shrines for all of Reebok's most prominent athletes—shrines complete with dramatic action photographs, their sports jerseys, and a pair of their signature shoes—and the halls are filled with so many young, determinedly athletic people that when I visited Reebok headquarters I suddenly wished I'd packed my gym clothes in case someone challenged me to wind sprints. At Stoughton, I met with a handful of the company's top designers and marketing executives in a long conference room on the third floor. In the course of two hours, they put one pair of shoes after another on the table in front of me, talking excitedly about each sneaker's prospects, because the feeling at Reebok is that things are finally turning around. The basketball shoe that Reebok brought out last winter for Allen Iverson, the star rookie guard for the Philadelphia 76ers, for example, is one of the hottest shoes in the country. Dr. Jay's sold out of Iversons in two days, compared with the week it took the store to sell out of Nike's new Air Jordans. Iverson himself is brash and charismatic and faster from foul line to foul line than anyone else in the league. He's the equivalent of those kids in the East Village who began wearing Hush Puppies way back when. He's an innovator, and the hope at Reebok is that if he gets big enough the whole company can ride back to coolness on his coattails, the way Nike rode to coolness on the coattails of Michael Jordan. That's why Baysie was so excited when the kid said Reebok was trying to get butter when he looked at the Rush and the DMX RXT: it was a sign, albeit a small one, that the indefinable, abstract thing called cool was coming back.

When Baysie comes back from a coolhunt, she sits down with 29 marketing experts and sales representatives and designers, and reconnects them to the street, making sure they have the right shoes going to the right places at the right price. When she got back from the Bronx, for example, the first thing she did was tell all these people they had to get a new men's DMX RXT out, fast, because the kids on the street loved the women's version. "It's hotter than we realized," she told them. The coolhunter's job in this instance is very specific. What DeeDee does, on the other hand, is a little more ambitious. With the L Report, she tries to construct a kind of grand matrix of cool, comprising not just shoes but everything kids like, and not just kids of certain East Coast urban markets but kids all over. DeeDee and her staff put it out four times a year, in six different versions—for New York, Los Angeles, San Francisco, Austin-Dallas, Seattle, and Chicago—and then sell it to manufacturers, retailers, and ad agencies (among others) for twenty thousand dollars a year. They go to each city and find the coolest bars and clubs, and ask the coolest kids to fill out questionnaires. The information is then divided into six categories—You Saw It Here First, Entertainment and Leisure, Clothing and Accessories, Personal and Individual, Aspirations, and Food and Beverages—which are, in turn, broken up into dozens of subcategories, so that Personal and Individual, for example, includes Cool Date, Cool Evening, Free Time, Favorite Possession, and on and on. The information in those subcategories is subdivided again by sex and by age bracket (14–18, 19–24, 25–30), and then, as a control, the L Report gives you the corresponding set of preferences for "mainstream" kids.

Few coolhunters bother to analyze trends with this degree of specificity. DeeDee's biggest competitor, for example, is something called the Hot Sheet, out of Manhattan. It uses a panel of three thousand kids a year from across the country and divides up their answers by sex and age, but it doesn't distinguish between regions, or between trendsetting and mainstream respondents. So what you're really getting is what all kids think is cool—not what cool kids think is cool, which is a considerably different piece of information. Janine Misdom and Joanne DeLuca, who run the Sputnik coolhunting group out of the garment district in Manhattan, meanwhile, favor an entirely impressionistic approach, sending out coolhunters with video cameras to talk to kids on the ground that it's too difficult to get cool kids to fill out questionnaires. Once, when I was visiting the Sputnik girls—as Misdom and DeLuca are known on the street, because they look alike and their first names are so similar and both have the same awesome New York accents—they showed me a video of the girl they believe was the patient zero of the whole eighties revival going on right now. It was back in September of 1993. Joanne and Janine were on Seventh Avenue, outside the Fashion Institute of Technology, doing random street interviews for a major jeans company, and, quite by accident, they ran into this nineteen-year-old raver. She had close-cropped hair, which was green at the top, and at the temples was shaved even closer and dyed pink. She had rings and studs all over her face, and a thick collection of silver tribal jewelry around her neck, and vintage jeans. She looked into the camera and said, "The sixties came in and then the seventies came in and I think it's ready to come back to the eighties. It's totally eighties: the eye makeup, the clothes. It's totally going back to that." Immediately, Joanne and Janine started asking around. "We talked to a few kids on the Lower East Side who said they were feeling the need to start breaking out their old Michael Jackson jackets," Joanne said. "They were joking about it. They weren't doing it yet. But they were going to, you know? They were saying, 'We're getting the urge to break out our Members Only jackets.'" That was right when Joanne and Janine were just starting up; calling the eighties revival was their first big break, and now they put out a full-blown videotaped report twice a year which is a collection of clips of interviews with extremely progressive people.

What DeeDee argues, though, is that cool is too subtle and too 31 variegated to be captured with these kind of broad strokes. Cool is a set of dialects, not a language. The L Report can tell you, for example, that nineteen-to-twenty-four-year-old male trendsetters in Seattle would most like to meet, among others, King Solomon and Dr. Seuss, and that nineteen-to-twenty-four-year-old female trendsetters in San Francisco have turned their backs on Calvin Klein, Nintendo Gameboy, and sex. What's cool right now? Among male New York trendsetters: North Face jackets, rubber and latex, khakis, and the rock band Kiss. Among female trendsetters: ska music, old-lady clothing, and cyber tech. In Chicago, snowboarding is huge among trendsetters of both sexes and all ages. Women over nineteen are into short hair, while those in their teens have embraced mod culture, rock climbing, tag watches, and bootleg pants. In Austin-Dallas, meanwhile, twenty-five-to-thirty-year-old women trendsetters are into hats, heroin, computers, cigars, Adidas, and velvet, while men in their twenties are into video games and hemp. In all, the typical L Report runs over one hundred pages. But with that flood of data comes an obsolescence disclaimer: "The fluctuating nature of the trendsetting market makes keeping up with trends a difficult task." By the spring, in other words, everything may have changed.

The key to coolhunting, then, is to look for cool people first and cool things later, and not the other way around. Since cool things are always changing, you can't look for them, because the very fact they are cool means you have no idea what to look for. What you would be doing is thinking back on what was cool before and extrapolating, which is about as useful as presuming that because the Dow rose ten points yesterday it will rise another ten points today. Cool people, on the other hand, are a constant.

When I was in California, I met Salvador Barbier, who had been described to me by a coolhunter as "the Michael Jordan of skateboarding." He was tall and lean and languid, with a cowboy's insouciance, and we drove through the streets of Long Beach at fifteen miles an hour in a white late-model Ford Mustang, a car he had bought as a kind of ironic status gesture ("It would look good if I had a Polo jacket or maybe Nautica," he said) to go with his '62 Econoline van and his '64 T-bird. Sal told me that he and his friends, who are all in their mid-twenties, recently took to dressing up as if they were in eighth grade again and gathering together—having a "rally"—on old BMX bicycles in front of their local 7-Eleven. "I'd wear muscle shirts, like Def Leppard or Foghat or some old heavy-metal band, and tight, tight tapered Levi's, and Vans on my feet—big, like, checkered Vans or striped Vans or camouflage Vans—and then wristbands and gloves with the fingers cut off. It was total eighties fashion. You had to look like that to participate in the rally. We had those denim jackets with patches on the back and combs that hung out the back pocket. We went without I.D.s, because we'd have to have someone else buy us beers." At this point, Sal laughed. He was driving really slowly and staring straight ahead and talking in a low drawl—the coolhunter's dream. "We'd ride to this bar and I'd have to carry my bike inside, because we have really expensive bikes, and when we got inside people would freak out. They'd say, 'Omigod,' and I was asking them if they wanted to go for a ride on the handlebars. They were like, 'What is wrong with you. My boyfriend used to dress like that in the eighth grade!' And I was like, 'He was probably a lot cooler then, too.'"

This is just the kind of person DeeDee wants. "I'm looking for somebody who is an individual, who has definitely set himself apart from everybody else, who doesn't look like his peers. I've run into trendsetters who look completely Joe Regular Guy. I can see Joe Regular Guy at a club listening to some totally hardcore band playing, and I say to myself 'Omigod, what's that guy doing here?' and that totally intrigues me, and I have to walk up to him and say, 'Hey, you're really into this band. What's up?' You know what I mean? I look at everything. If I see Joe Regular Guy sitting in a coffee shop and everyone around him has blue hair, I'm going to gravitate toward him, because, hey, what's Joe Regular Guy doing in a coffee shop with people with blue hair?"

We were sitting outside the Fred Segal store in West Hollywood. 5 I was wearing a very conservative white Brooks Brothers button-down and a pair of Levi's, and DeeDee looked first at my shirt and then my pants and dissolved into laughter: "I mean, I might even go up to you in a cool place."

Picking the right person is harder than it sounds, though. Piney 36 Kahn, who works for DeeDee, says, "There are a lot of people in the gray area. You've got these kids who dress ultra funky and have their own style. Then you realize they're just running after their friends." The trick is not just to be able to tell who is different but to be able to tell when that difference represents something truly cool. It's a gut thing. You have to somehow just know. DeeDee hired Piney because Piney clearly knows: she is twenty-four and used to work with the Beastie Boys and has the formidable self-possession of someone who is not only cool herself but whose parents were cool. "I mean," she says, "they named me after a tree."

Piney and DeeDee said that they once tried to hire someone as a 37 coolhunter who was not, himself, cool, and it was a disaster.

"You can give them the boundaries," Piney explained. "You can 38 say that if people shop at Banana Republic and listen to Alanis Morissette they're probably not trendsetters. But then they might go out and assume that everyone who does that is not a trendsetter, and not look at the other things."

"I mean, I myself might go into Banana Republic and buy a 39 T-shirt," DeeDee chimed in.

Their non-cool coolhunter just didn't have that certain instinct, 40 that sense that told him when it was O.K. to deviate from the manual. Because he wasn't cool, he didn't know cool, and that's the essence of the third rule of cool: you have to be one to know one. That's why Baysie is still on top of this business at forty-one. "It's easier for me to tell you what kid is cool than to tell you what things are cool," she says. But that's all she needs to know. In this sense, the third rule of cool fits perfectly into the second: the second rule says that cool cannot be manufactured, only observed, and the third says that it can only be observed by those who are themselves cool. And, of course, the first rule says that it cannot accurately be observed at all, because the act of discovering cool causes cool to take flight, so if you add all three together they describe a closed loop, the hermeneutic circle of coolhunting, a phenomenon whereby not only can the uncool not see cool but cool cannot even be adequately described to them. Baysie says that she can see a coat on one of her friends and think it's not cool but then see the same coat on DeeDee and think that it is cool. It is not possible to be cool, in other words, unless you are—in some larger sense—already cool, and so the phenomenon that the uncool cannot see and cannot have described to them is also something that they cannot ever attain, because if they did it would no longer be cool. Coolhunting represents the ascendancy, in the marketplace, of high school.

Once, I was visiting DeeDee at her house in Laurel Canyon when 41 one of her L Report assistants, Jonas Vail, walked in. He'd just come back from Niketown on Wilshire Boulevard, where he'd bought seven hundred dollars' worth of the latest sneakers to go with the three hundred dollars' worth of skateboard shoes he'd bought earlier in the afternoon. Jonas is tall and expressionless, with a peacoat, dark jeans, and short-cropped black hair. "Jonas is good," DeeDee says. "He works with me on everything. That guy knows more pop culture. You know: What was the name of the store Mrs. Garrett owned on 'The Facts of Life'? He knows all the names of the extras from eighties sitcoms. I can't believe someone like him exists. He's fucking unbelievable. Jonas can spot a cool person a mile away."

Jonas takes the boxes of shoes and starts unpacking them on the 42 couch next to DeeDee. He picks up a pair of the new Nike ACG hiking boots, and says, "All the Japanese in Niketown were really into these." He hands the shoes to DeeDee.

"Of *course* they were!" she says. "The Japanese are all into the 43 tech-looking shit. Look how exaggerated it is, how bulbous." DeeDee has very ambivalent feelings about Nike, because she thinks its marketing has got out of hand. When she was in the New York Niketown with a girlfriend recently, she says, she started getting light-headed and freaked out. "It's cult, cult, cult. It was like, 'Hello, are we all drinking the Kool-Aid here?'" But this shoe she loves. It's Dr. Jay's in the Bronx all over again. DeeDee turns the shoe around and around in the air, tapping the big clear-blue plastic bubble on the side—the visible Air-Sole unit—with one finger. "It's so fucking rad. It looks like a platypus!" In front of me, there is a pair of Nike's new shoes for the basketball player Jason Kidd.

I pick it up. "This looks . . . cool," I venture uncertainly. 44

DeeDee is on the couch, where she's surrounded by shoeboxes 45 and sneakers and white tissue paper, and she looks up reprovingly because, of course, I don't get it. I can't get it. "Beyooond cool, Maalcolm. Beyooond cool."

SALESPEAK

Roy Fox

No profit whatsoever can possibly be made but at the expense of another.

—Michel de Montaigne, "Of Liars," 1580

WHAT IS SALESPEAK?

Salespeak is any type of message surrounding a transaction between people. First, Salespeak is persuasive in nature. It can convince us to purchase products and services. It can also persuade us, directly and indirectly, to "buy into" political candidates, beliefs, ideologies, attitudes, values, and lifestyles. Salespeak persuades by presenting us with facts, where logic, language, and numbers dominate the message. More often, though, it persuades by massaging us—entertaining and arousing us, and changing our emotions with imagery, sound effects, and music.

Second, Salespeak can function as a type of entertainment or escapism—as an end in itself, where we are more focused on the experiences surrounding consumerism (e.g., browsing through an L. L. Bean catalog) than we are on actually purchasing something. Salespeak occurs when messages are crafted so as to "hit" a specific, "targeted" audience. Therefore, Salespeakers collect and analyze information about their audiences to help them shape their messages.

Third, Salespeak usually employs a systematic approach in targeting its audience. A theme for Boltz laundry detergent, such as, "It's white as lightning!" might unify different types of messages communicated through different channels. The goal here is to create "overlapping fields of experience" (Ray 1982), hitting us from several sides in different ways, in short, to create an "environment" of persuasion. In this chapter, Salespeak also includes any type of message about transactions between people, such as a market report describing a specific group of consumers.

We live in a market-driven economy in which we consume more than we produce. It's little wonder, then, that Salespeak flows constantly—from television, billboards, print ads, and blinking Internet messages. Because Salespeak touches nearly every area of life, its infinite tones and painstakingly crafted imagery appear in an endless variety of forms. Salespeak ranges from the hard-sell radio pitch of the local Ford dealer to the vague, soft, amorphous TV commercial that merely wants you to know that the good folks at Exxon care.

Salespeak includes the envelope in your mailbox that states, "God's Holy Spirit said, 'Someone connected with this address needs this help.'" Salespeak ranges from the on-screen commercial loops playing on the ATM machine while you wait for your cash, to the plugs for car washes that appear on the screens affixed to the gas pump as you fill up your car. Salespeak even shows up in slot machines designed to entice children (Glionna 1999). These slots for tots now feature themes such as Candyland, Monopoly, the Three Stooges, the Pink Panther, and South Park. This is the gaming industry's attempt to promote a "family-friendly" image, which will help ensure that future generations will support the casino industry (Ruskin 1999). Salespeak also sprouts from the "product information" about a new computer embedded within the instructions for installing a software program, from the camera shot in a popular film that lingers on a bag of Frito's corn chips, and from the large sign inside Russia's *Mir* space station that states, "Even in Space . . . Pepsi is Changing the Script." Salespeak is indeed the script, on earth as it is in heaven.

A DAY IN THE LIFE

At 6:03 A.M., Mrs. Anderson's voice comes over the intercom into her teenaged daughter's bedroom. Mrs. Anderson asks, "Pepsi? It's time to wake up, dear. Pehhhp-si . . . are you up and moving?"

Pepsi answers groggily, "Yeah . . . I'm up. Morning, Mom." As Pepsi sits up in bed, she reaches over and hits the button on her old pink Barbie alarm clock, which rests on her old American Girl traditional oak jewelry box. As both cherished items catch her eye, she pauses and wistfully recalls those happy days of girlhood, rubbing her hand over the *Little Mermaid* bedsheet. If only she hadn't given away her favorite purple My Little Pony to her best childhood friend, Microsoft McKenzie, who lives next door.

Just then her mother's voice calls her back to reality, "Good deal, sweetie. Let me know when you finish your shower. I just got your Gap sweatshirt out of the dryer, but I couldn't get that Gatorade stain out of your Tommy Hilfiger pants, so I'm washing them again."

Once upstairs, Pepsi sits down for a bowl of Cap'n Crunch cereal. ⁹
She peels a banana, carefully pulling off a bright yellow sticker, which
states, "ABC. Zero calories." She places the used sticker onto her
McDonald's book cover. Pepsi's younger brother, Nike, dressed in his
Babylon Five T-shirt, places a Star Trek notebook into his Star Wars
book bag as he intently watches the Amoco morning newscast on the
video wall. The network anchor tells about the latest corporate merger
as he reads from his perch within the "N" of the giant MSNBC logo.
Then Mrs. Anderson walks into the nutrition pod.

Mrs. Anderson: Hey, Peps, what's going on at school today?
*Pepsi:*Nothing much. Just gotta finish that dumb science
    experiment.
"Mrs. Anderson: Which one is that?
Pepsi: That one called "Digging for Data." We learned about
    scientific inquiry stuff and how to deduce conclusions.
    We learned that American settlers were short because
    they didn't eat enough meat and stuff like that.
Mrs. Anderson: Oh, yes! That was one of my favorites when I
    was in school. Those National Livestock and Meat Board
    teaching kits are wonderful! I liked it even better than
    Campbell Soup's "Prego Thickness Experiment." How
    'bout you?
Pepsi: I dunno. Everyone already knows that Prego spaghetti
    sauce is three times thicker and richer than Ragu's sauce.
Mrs. Anderson: Well, yes, of course they do. But that's not the
    only point. There are larger goals here, namely, your
    becoming the best high-volume consumer possible. Isn't
    that right, dear?
Pepsi: Yeah, I guess so.

Pepsi's school bus, equipped with the latest electronic wrap- ¹⁰
around billboard, mentions that the price of Chocolate Cheetah
Crunch "is being sliced as you read this—down to $48.95 per ten-
pounder!" Pepsi takes her seat and discusses this price reduction
with her locker partner, Reebok Robinson. They engage in a lively
conversation about which of them loves Cheetah Crunch more. Next,
the screen on the back of the seat in front of them catches their attention: a large dancing lamb sings, "Be there! Tonight only! At the IBM
Mall! All remaining Rickon collectibles must go! Pledge bidding
only! Be there!" Even Reebok cannot contain a squeal.

At school, Pepsi watches Channel One, the National Truth 11 Channel, during her first three classes. The first news story documents the precise steps in which Zestra, the new star of the Z-5 Lectradisk corporate communication spots, went about purchasing her new video wall unit. Afterward, Pepsi and her peers receive biofeedback printouts of their responses registered during this program via the reaction console on their desks. Next, the students use voice-print technology to describe what they were feeling during the broadcast.

Then their teacher, Ms. Qualcomm, tells them to take a twenty- 12 minute recess at the Commoditarium before they return for Tech Lab, where they will begin the unit "Product Scanning: Art or Science?" At the Commoditarium, Pepsi purchases one bag of Kwizzee sticks, one can of Channel One soda, and a One-der Bar, in addition to a pair of Golden Arch earrings she can't live without. The accessories for the earrings, which she also longs for, will have to wait.

Back at Tech Lab, Pepsi and her peers receive a half hour of 13 AT&T ("Allotted Time & Testing," sponsored by AT&T, in which students are free to explore their own interests on the GodNet). In the upper-left corner of her computer screen, Pepsi watches what appears to be an enlarged part of human anatomy, alternately shrinking and enlarging, as one of her favorite new songs beats in sync. The olfactory port of her computer emits a musky odor. In the background of this pulsating image, sticks of lightning flare randomly against a deep blue sky. Pepsi looks at them more closely and detects that each one contains three small letters: A, T, and T. She smiles, points, and clicks on the window.

Immediately, this message forms on screen in large, puffy blue let- 14 ters: "A, T, & T Loves You." Then the message begins dissolving and enlarging simultaneously, so that the background is now the same blue as the message. Huge lips fill the screen. Pepsi is unsure whether they are the lips of a man or woman. The lips slowly murmur, "You, Pepsi . . . You're the one . . . Oh, yes . . . Nobody else. Just you."

Pepsi, mesmerized, half whispers to herself, "Me?" as the lips 15 fade at the same time that the blue background re-forms into the previous message, "A, T, & T Loves You." Pepsi clicks again. Three golden books appear on screen. One is titled "A, T, & T's Pledge to You, Pepsi Anderson." Another one is titled, "Making Love Rich," and the third is titled, "Us . . . Forever." The lights of the Tech Lab dim, signaling students that it's time to begin their new unit. The lights slowly fade out until the lab is nearly dark. Pepsi hears muffled patriotic music from the opposite side of the room—a flute and drum, playing the tune of "Yankee Doodle Dandy." From the far end of the ceiling, an image of the traditional "fyfe and drum corps"—the three ragged soldiers in Revolutionary Army garb—come marching across the screen; above the U.S. flag flies a larger one, with a golden arch on it.

As the tattered trio exit via a slow dissolve on the opposite end 16 of the ceiling screen, the room goes completely dark. Pepsi twists her head and limbers up, as her classmates do, almost in unison. Then, on instinct, Pepsi and her peers look upward to the neon green and pink Laser Note swirling above them: "To thine own self, be blue. And rakest thou joy into thine own taste sphere! Tru-Blu Vervo Dots: now half price at Commoditarium!" A laser image of Shakespeare forms from the dissolving lights. Next, the bard's face dissolves into blue Vervo Dots. Pepsi, feeling vaguely tired and hungry, saves her place on screen so she can return later to find out what's in the three golden books. Before she exits, she is automatically transferred to another screen so that she can input her biofeedback prints from the past half hour.

At home that night, Pepsi and her family gather in the Recipient 17 Well. To activate the video wall, Mrs. Anderson submits a forehead print on the ConsumaScan. Before any audio can be heard, a Nike logo appears on the screen for two minutes. Mrs. Anderson turns to her daughter.

> *Mrs. Anderson:* So, Peps, you were awfully quiet at dinner. Are you okay? Everything all right at school?
>
> *Pepsi:* Fine. I just get tired of learning all the time.
>
> *Mrs. Anderson (sighing):* Well, sweetie, I know. Things are so much different nowadays than when I was your age. You kids have to work harder in school because there are so many more products and services to keep up with.
>
> *Pepsi:* Yeah, I guess so. . . .
>
> *Mrs. Anderson:* But you've also got many luxuries we never had. Why, when I was born, parents were completely ignorant about giving their children beautiful names. My family just called me "Jennifer." Ugh! Can you believe it?
>
> *Pepsi:* Oh, gag me, Mom! "Jennifer"?! You're kidding! How did you and Dad name me?
>
> *Mrs. Anderson:* Well, let's see. . . . We first fell in love with your name when Pepsico offered us a lifetime membership at the Nova Health Spa if we'd name you "Pepsi." I

thought it was so refreshing—not to mention thirst quenching and tasty. Besides—it's your generation!

Pepsi: And I'll always love you and Dad for bestowing me with eternal brandness. . .

Mrs. Anderson: It's just because we love you, that's all. Growing up branded is a lot easier these days—especially after the Renaissance of 2008, just after you were born.

Pepsi: What was that?

Mrs. Anderson: You know—*life cells!* We got them a few years after the Second Great Brand Cleansing War.

Pepsi: But I thought we always had life cells, that we were just born with 'em. . . .

Mrs. Anderson: My gosh, no, girl! When I was your age we had to stay glued to National Public Radio to keep up with the latest fluctuations of the NASDAQ and high tech markets.

Pepsi: Jeez . . . I can't imagine life without life cells.

Mrs. Anderson: Me either—now! Back then, it all started with Moletronics and the first conversions of Wall Street data-streams into what they used to call "subcutaneous pseudo-neurons." But that's ancient history for you!

Pepsi: Mom?

Mrs. Anderson: Yes, dear?

Pepsi: Can we set aside some special family time, so we can talk about that relationship portfolio with AT&T?

Mrs. Anderson: Well, of course! Maybe during spring break at the cabin? That's not the kind of thing we ever want to slight.

At this moment, the video wall's audio activates. The Nike [18] swoosh logo forms into a running cheetah as a male voice-over states, "Nike Leopard-Tech Laser Runners. Be the Cheetah you were born free to be." Mrs. Anderson turns back to her daughter and asks, "Would you mind running to the Pantry Pod and seeing if there's any more of that Chocolate Cheetah Crunch left?" "Sure," says Pepsi, turning as she leaves the room, *If* we can talk about those new shoes I need." . . .

IS PEPSI'S WORLD ALREADY HERE?

Yes. Most of what happens to Pepsi in this scenario is based on fact. [19] A few other parts are extensions or exaggerations of what already occurs in everyday life. Let's begin with a girl named Pepsi. In Pepsi's world of Salespeak, nearly every facet of life is somehow linked to sales. Pepsi, the girl, lives in a Pepsi world, where person, product, and hype have merged with everyday life.

Salespeak is all-powerful. As small children, as soon as we 20 become aware that a world exists outside of ourselves, we become a "targeted audience." From then on, we think in the voices of Salespeak. We hear them, we see them. We smell them, taste them, touch them, dream them, become them. Salespeak is often targeted at young people, the group marketers most prize because first, they spend "disposable" income, as well as influence how their parents spend money (see the following section, "Notes from the World of Salespeak"); second, people tend to establish loyalties to certain brands early in life; and third, young people are more likely to buy items on impulse. For these reasons and more, Salespeak is most prevalent and vivid for children and young adults. Hence, most of this chapter focuses on the layers of Salespeak that surround these groups. The core issue is targeting kids in the first place, regardless of the product being sold.

What's in a Name?

At this writing, I've neither read nor heard of a human being 21 legally named after a product or service (though I feel certain that he or she is out there). I have, though, heard that school administrators in Plymouth, Michigan, are considering auctioning off school names to the highest bidder. It's only a matter of time before kids attend "Taco Bell Middle School" or "Gap Kids Elementary School" (Labi 1999). Appropriating names—and hence identities—is essentially an act of aggression, of control over others' personal identity. Our practice of naming things for commercial purposes is not new. Consider San Diego's Qualcomm Stadium. Unlike St. Louis's Busch Stadium or Denver's Coors Field, the name Qualcomm has no connections to people or things already traditionally linked with baseball. In Pepsi's world, "AT&T" stood for "Allotted Time for Testing." To my knowledge, commercial or corporate names have yet to be used for identifying processes. However, they have been used to identify specific places where educational processes occur.

For example, the Derby, Kansas, school district named its ele- 22 mentary school resource center the GenerationNext Center. The district agreed to use the Pepsi slogan to name their new facility, as well as to serve only Pepsi products, in exchange for one million dollars

(Perrin 1997, 1A). Even ice cream is now named so that it can advertise something else: the name of Ben and Jerry's butter almond ice cream is called "Dilbert's World: Totally Nuts" (Solomon 1998a).

Every time we see or read or hear a commercial name, an 23 "impression" registers. Advertising profits depend on the type and number of impressions made by each ad message. Therefore, Pepsi Anderson and her friend, Microsoft McKenzie, are walking, breathing, random ad messages. (Similar important names) are now devised solely for purposes of advertising. Nothing more. Such names become ads. In earlier times and in other cultures, as well as our own, names were sacred: they communicated the essence of our identity, not just to others but to ourselves as well. To rob someone of her name was to appropriate her identity, to deny her existence. In *I Know Why the Caged Bird Sings,* Maya Angelou speaks of how demoralizing it was for African Americans to be "called out of name" by white people, who would refer to any African American male as "boy," "Tom," or "Uncle."

Similarly, several years ago, the rock musician and composer 24 known as Prince changed his name to a purely graphic symbol. The result, of course, was that nobody could even pronounce it! By default he became known as "The Artist Formerly Known as Prince." In an interview on MTV, this musician-composer explained that the public believed he was crazy because print and electronic media had proclaimed him so, over and over. He therefore changed his name to something unpronounceable to halt this labeling. It worked. In effect, this man regained control of his own life because he found a way to stop others from controlling it for him, as they were doing by writing about him in the media. This man understands the general semantics principle that the word is not the thing symbolized—that the map is not the territory. . . .

The long-term effects of replacing real names with commercial 25 labels (of important spaces, processes, and possibly even people) can benefit nobody except those doing the appropriating—those reaping revenue from increased sales. At the very least, this practice demonstrates, in concrete, definitive ways, that we value materialism and the act of selling above all else.

Celebrating Coke Day at the Carbonated Beverage Company

At century's end, the question is not "Where and when does 26 Salespeak appear?" Rather, the real question is, "Where and when does Salespeak *not* appear?" Only in churches and other places of worship? (Not counting, of course, the church that advertised itself by proclaiming on its outside message board: "Come in for a faith lift.") Salespeak is more than a voice we hear and see: we also wear it, smell it, touch it, play with it. Ads on book covers, notebooks, backpacks, pencils, and pens are common. So are the girl Pepsi's Gap sweatshirt, Tommy Hilfiger pants, Barbie alarm clock, and *Little Mermaid* bedsheets. The bulletins that Pepsi and her classmates received about current sales are also authentic: PepsiCo has offered free beepers to teens, who are periodically contacted with updated ad messages.

Salespeak is seeping into the smallest crevices of American life.   27
As you fill your car with gas, you can now watch commercials on a small screen on the gas pump. As you wait for your transaction at the ATM machine, you can view commercials. As you wait in the switch-back line at an amusement park, you can watch commercials on several screens. As you wait in your doctor's office, you can read about medicines to buy, as well as watch commercials for them. As you stand in line at Wal-Mart's customer service desk, you can watch ads for Wal-Mart on a huge screen before you. As you wait for the phone to ring when making a long-distance call, you'll hear a soft, musical tinkle, followed by a velvety voice that intones, "AT&T."

As your children board their school bus, you'll see ads wrapped   28
around it. When you pick up a bunch of bananas in the grocery store, like our friend Pepsi in the earlier scenario, you may have to peel off yellow stickers that state, "ABC. Zero calories." When you call a certain school in Texas and don't get an answer, you'll hear this recorded message: "Welcome to the Grapevine-Colleyville Independent School District, where we are proudly sponsored by the Dr. Pepper Bottling Company of Texas" (Perrin 1997).

Salespeak also commonly appears under the guise of school   29
"curriculum"—from formal business-education partnerships, to free teacher workshops provided to introduce new textbooks. Corporate-produced "instructional materials" are sometimes thinly veiled sales pitches that can distort the truth. The curriculum unit "Digging for Data" mentioned earlier as part of Pepsi's school day, is actual material used in schools.

For another "learning experience," students were assigned to be   30
"quality control technicians" as they completed "The Carbonated Beverage Company" unit, provided free to schools by PepsiCo. Students taste-tested colas, analyzed cola samples, took video tours of the St. Louis Pepsi plant, and visited a local Pepsi plant (Bingham 1998, 1A). Ads have even appeared in math textbooks. *Mathematics:*

Applications and Connections, published by McGraw-Hill, and used in middle schools, includes problems that are just as much about advertising as they are arithmetic—salespeak masquerading as education. Here's a sample decimal division problem: "Will is saving his allowance to buy a pair of Nike shoes that cost $68.25. If Will earns $3.25 per week, how many weeks will Will need to save?" Directly next to this problem is a full-color picture of a pair of Nike shoes (Hays 1999). The 1999 edition of this book contains the following problem: "The best-selling packaged cookie in the world is the Oreo cookie. The diameter of the Oreo cookie is 1.75 inches. Express the diameter of an Oreo cookie as a fraction in simplest form." It seems no accident that "Oreo" is repeated three times in this brief message; repetition is an ancient device used in propaganda and advertising. More insidious is the fact that such textbooks present the act of saving money for Nike shoes as a *natural* state of affairs, a given in life. Requiring captive audiences of kids to interact with brand names in such mentally active ways helps ensure product-identification and brand-name loyalty during kids' future years as consumers.

Some schools slavishly serve their corporate sponsors. After sealing a deal with Coca-Cola, a school in Georgia implemented an official "Coke Day" devoted to celebrating Coca-Cola products. On that day, Mike Cameron, a senior at the school, chose to exercise his right to think by wearing a T-shirt bearing the Pepsi logo. He was promptly suspended ("This School Is Brought to You By: Cola? Sneakers?" 1998, 11A).   31

This intense focus on selling products to a captive audience of students is illustrated by the following letter sent to District 11's school principals in Colorado Springs, Colorado. The letter was written by the district's executive director of "school leadership." In September 1997, the district had signed an $8 million contract with Coca-Cola (Labi 1999).   32

Dear Principal:

Here we are in year two of the great Coke contract . . . .

First, the good news: This year's installment from Coke is "in the house," and checks will be cut for you to pick up in my office this week. Your share will be the same as last year.

Elementary School	$3,000
Middle School	$15,000
High School	$25,000

Now the not-so-good news: we must sell 70,000 cases of product (including juices, sodas, waters, etc.) at least once during the first three years of the contract. If we reach this goal, your school allotments will be guaranteed for the next seven years.

The math on how to achieve this is really quite simple. Last year we had 32,439 students, 3,000 employees, and 176 days in the school year. If 35,439 staff and students buy one Coke product every other day for a school year, we will double the required quota.

Here is how we can do it:

1. Allow students to purchase and consume vended products throughout the day.
2. Locate machines where they are accessible to the students all day. Research shows that vender purchases are closely linked to availability. Location, location, location is the key. You may have as many machines as you can handle. Pueblo Central High tripled its volume of sales by placing vending machines on all three levels of the school. The Coke people surveyed the middle and high schools this summer and have suggestions on where to place additional machines.
3. A list of Coke products is enclosed to allow you to select from the entire menu of beverages. Let me know which products you want, and we will get them in. Please let me know if you need electrical outlets.
4. A calendar of promotional events is enclosed to help you advertise Coke products.

I know this is "just one more thing from downtown," but the long-term benefits are worth it.

Thanks for your help.

> John Bushey
> The Coke Dude
> (Bushey 1998)

With visionary leaders such as "The Coke Dude" to inspire 33 them, students will be well prepared to perpetuate a world ruled by Salespeak. Of course, Pepsi (the girl), Mike (the actual student expelled for wearing a Pepsi T-shirt), and their fellow students did not begin encountering ads in high school. It begins much earlier. . .

The National Truth Channel

Many other details of Pepsi's day are anchored in fact, not fiction. 34
In Pepsi's not-too-distant world, Channel One television has become
the "National Truth Channel." Today Channel One, owned by a private corporation, beams daily commercials to more than 8 million
American kids attending middle schools and high schools. It therefore imposes more uniformity on public school kids and their curriculum than the federal government ever has. For all practical
purposes, it has indeed been our "national" channel for several years.

Although I made up the "Truth" part of "The National Truth 35
Channel," I want to note that it serves as Doublespeak nested within
Salespeak—a common occurrence in real life. For example, the term
"corporate communication" (used in Pepsi's world, above, to refer to
commercials) is a euphemism that the Benetton company actually
used to refer to its ads. And although laser ads have yet to appear on
the ceilings of classrooms, as they do in Pepsi's world, it is true that
a few years ago, a company wanted to launch into geosynchronous
orbit a massive panel that could be emblazoned with a gigantic corporate logo, visible for periods of time, over certain cities (Doheny-
Farina 1999). Here, the promise of reality far exceeds what happened
in Pepsi's fictional classroom.

Also, remember that "news story" about Zestra, a star of "corpo- 36
rate communication" spots that Pepsi watched on Channel One?
More truth than fiction here, too. Since 1989, Channel One has sometimes blurred the lines between news, commercials, and public service announcements. In one study (Fox 1996), many students mistook
commercials for news programs or public service announcements,
such as those that warn viewers about drunk driving. The result was
that students knew the product being advertised and regarded it
warmly because, as one student told me, "They [the manufacturers
and advertisers] are trying to do good. They care about us."

In the worst case of such blurring that I observed during the two- 37
year period of this study, the students could hardly be faulted.
Instead, the Salespeak was highly deceptive (merging with
Doublespeak). That is, PepsiCo's series of ads called "It's Like This"
were designed to look very much like documentary news footage
and public service announcements. The actors spoke directly into the
swinging, handheld camera, as if they were being interviewed; the
ads were filmed in black and white, and the product's name was
never spoken by any of the people in the commercial, although the

rapid-fire editing included brief shots of the Pepsi logo, in color, on signs and on merchandise.

Just as in Pepsi's world, described earlier in this chapter, real-life 38 ads are often embedded within programs, as well as other commercials, products, instructions, and even "transitional spaces" between one media message and another. For example, when the girl Pepsi took a break from her "learning," she went to the school's Commoditarium, or mini-mall, to shop for items that had been advertised at school. Again, there is truth here. Although schools do not yet contain mini-malls, they do contain stores and increasing numbers of strategically placed vending machines. A ninth-grade girl told me that after students viewed Channel One in the morning and watched commercials for M&Ms candies, her teacher allowed them to take a break. The student said she'd often walk down the hall and purchase M&Ms from the vending machine. In such schools, operant conditioning is alive and well. This is not the only way in which many schools are emulating shopping malls. My daughter's high school cafeteria is a "food court," complete with McDonald's and Pizza Hut.

By establishing itself in public schools, Channel One automati- 39 cally "delivers" a captive, well-defined audience to its advertisers, more than was ever possible before. "Know thy audience"—as specifically as possible—is the name of the advertising game. Marketers have become increasingly effective at obtaining all kinds of demographic and psychographic information on consumers. Channel One increasingly hones its messages based on the constant flow of demographic information it extracts from viewers, often under the guise of "clubs" and contests, which seek information on individuals, teams, classes, and entire schools ("Be a Channel One School"). Channel One's printed viewing and "curriculum" guides for teachers, as well as its Web site for students, also constantly solicit marketing information.

It's a Wonderful Day in the "Branded, Private Electronic Neighborhood"

Pepsi went to her computer lab to work and quickly drifted into 40 an ethereal world of good-vibes Salespeak, which "interacted" with her in informal and personal ways. She was electronically massaged and called by name. Consumers interacting with advertisers, one-on-one, is the marketer's nirvana. This, too, already happens. Like the Salespeakers who use television, cyber-entrepreneurs are eager to use computers to spread Salespeak. They are equally excited about using computers to "track" consumers for collecting ever more specific and detailed psychographics—who we are, what we fantasize, what we do—for purposes of selling. One computer company plans to give away approximately 1 million computers in exchange for users who would be "willing to disclose their interests, income, and on-line browsing habits" ("Free Computers Offered by Fledgling Company," *Columbia* [Missouri] *Daily Tribune,* February 9, 1999, 7B). The company monitors the sites that users visit and the ads they click on (from a screen never devoid of ads). If users don't dial up to the Internet often enough, new ads are sent automatically to the computer terminal.

Although today's schools aren't yet as high-tech as Pepsi's school 41 (which used "ConsumaScans" and "forehead prints" to analyze her responses to media), such approaches are not far-fetched. For example, market researchers now work directly in some schools, to determine "what sparks kids." One marketing company conducts focus groups in schools on behalf of Kentucky Fried Chicken, McDonald's, and Mattel Toys—all to improve advertising to kids (Labi 1999). To date, the most ambitious marketing venture is ZapMe! Corporation's offer of entire computer labs, fast servers with satellite connection, teacher training, and other lollipops to public and private schools, all for "free." The only price for this feast is that the systems will contain advertising and market research technology, in all its interactive and multimedia glory. However, the ZapMe! Corporation folks don't dare call it advertising. Instead they call it "brand imaging spots" and "dedicated branding spaces." Ah, Salespeak.

To date, 9,000 schools have signed up for this scheme, which is 42 being piloted in several California schools. The ZapMe! approach is strikingly similar to Channel One television. In exchange for delivering this massive audience, schools receive some equipment from Channel One—monitors, a satellite dish (capable of picking up only Channel One's signal) and other equipment amounting to a total of about $50,000. Hence, it's hardly a shock that Channel One is found most often in low-income communities (McCarthy 1993, 4A).

ZapMe! President Frank Vigil tried to distinguish his company 43 from Channel One: "Channel One is television. What we are is really an interactive learning tool, so we're very, very different" (Chmielewski 1998). Of course the Internet differs from TV. We've long known that when people interact with texts, they improve their retention and learning, internalizing those messages more quickly and deeply. ZapMe! wants to use this power to sell stuff. In addition to the constantly moving billboard on the screen, and in addition to the tracking of students for market research purposes, students are further immersed in ad culture when they collect "ZapPoints," which they can spend at an e-commerce mall.

Billions and Billions of Buyers and Bucks. You might think 44 that the $50,000 worth of video equipment that schools receive from Channel One in exchange for their delivering audiences seems almost a decent tradeoff, especially to poorer schools—but only until you consider that Channel One can charge advertisers as much as $200,000 for one 30-second ad (Hoynes 1997). Such sales pile up to an estimated $600,000 per day for Channel One (New York State Department of Education memo, May 23, 1995). The Internet ZapMe! Corporation, however, wants more than this. Much more. According to its Web site, ZapMe! will reach "a potential audience exceeding 50 million students in the United States and over a billion students worldwide." Sherman's march on Atlanta, the Allied landing in Normandy, and ZapMe!'s ad blitz into the world's classrooms. Ah, what progress democracy maketh.

The other "benefit" of beaming Channel One television into the 45 schools is supposed to be its news program. However, research has concluded that Channel One news contains precious little news. The bulk of each broadcast (80 percent according to one study) is devoted to "advertising, sports, weather and natural disasters, features and profiles, and self-promotion of Channel One" (Honan 1997). Nobody in the schools can preview these daily broadcasts, because the signals are received inside of a locked metal box. And nobody at the schools has a key to open this box. Similarly, according to a press release from Commercial Alert (October 29, 1998), ZapMe! computers will contain "banner ads built into the browser interface" of their Internet access. Hence, nobody in the school can tamper with it. This is the state of democratic education.

Hitting Heads with Two-by-Four Billboards. Students using 46 ZapMe! computers must view advertising on their computer screens. One direct use of ads is ZapMe!'s "dynamic billboard," a two-by-four-inch rectangle in the screen's lower left corner. Ad logos and messages now rotate, but these "dynamic" appeals will likely escalate to video, audio, and other whiz-bangs because, well, ads try to attract attention. Schools will be required to have students use ZapMe! computer labs at least four hours per day.

This is similar to Channel One's requirement, that schools must 47 submit attendance records to guarantee that the program is aired during 90 percent of the school days, in at least 80 percent of the classrooms. Don't forget that every state has compulsory school attendance laws, which literally force kids to receive such messages. Also, Channel One costs taxpayers an estimated $1.8 billion annually in lost instructional time—$300 million of this to ads (Center for Commercial-Free Education, November 16, 1998). In short, taxpayers have already paid for this time that's being sold to advertisers. Channel One has convinced me that beaming glitzy ads to captive kids is highly effective. When kids see a specific item on TV at school, they often assume that the school itself endorses the product. Channel One has also broadcast commercials that closely resemble documentaries, causing kids (and adults) to blur ads with more non-biased messages. Not only are many of the same commercials repeated endlessly, but kids also "replay" commercials themselves in a variety of ways—from singing the jingles, to repeating dialogue, to creating art projects that mirror products and product messages. Some kids even dream about commercials. In short, schools become echo chambers for ad messages. We should not be surprised, then, that such environments affect kids' behavior, including their consumer behavior (Fox 1996).

$pinning $ales in "Uncluttered Environments."   Like Channel 48 One, ZapMe! is motivated by what it calls an "open" or "uncluttered" market, one free of the usual teen "distractions" of family, music, television, jobs, and cars. An "uncluttered" environment also means little or no resistance to the values and ideologies (e.g., materialism, competition) contained in most ads. If you have doubts about these corporations' intentions, linger a little while over their lingo. For example, in a press release, Martin Grant, Channel One's president of sales and marketing, said, "Channel One is a marketer's secret weapon. When used creatively by today's innovative marketers, it is an unparalleled way to reach a massive teen audience in a highly relevant, important, and uncluttered environment" (August 9, 1995). Another marketer once referred to in-school ads as "brand and product loyalties through classroom-centered, peer-powered lifestyle patterning." Translation: get 'em while they're young, captive, and have disposable income.

And consider this excerpt from the ZapMe! Web site: "Using fast 49 and reliable satellite communications, we can create new methods of training, education, *sales* and even the *buying and selling of services and products.* Distance training, software distribution and high bandwidth data distribution are some of the exciting applications unfolding in the *global services market.* Join us in our pursuit of *expanding the market* by creating *complete application solutions"* (ZapMe! Web site n.d., italics added).

In the eyes (and prose) of this writer, dollar signs spin like wheels ⁵⁰ of fire on the Fourth of July. Just within the first sentence, sales are mentioned twice, and sales is what the sentence ends with, thereby emphasizing it most. And although "complete application solutions" includes more than sales, it certainly implies that sales will always be there (if not, entrepreneurs would not consider it "complete").

Living and Learning in the "Branded, Private Electronic Neighborhood"

Other, less visible problems occur when Salespeak invades ⁵¹ schools. For instance, these two corporations "standardize" public education in ways that most of us never intended. Today, our most common or core curriculum in American education is the television commercial. More students watch ads for Bubblicious Bubble Gum than read Dickens's *A Tale of Two Cities*.

And now, ZapMe! executives promise Internet and cultural ⁵² homogeneity for the thousands of schools that sign on with them. "Reduce Undesirable Websites!" they proclaim, because "in the ZapMe! Intranet environment, students [sic] access to undesirable websites is virtually eliminated." ZapMe! further assures us that "customized browser with search functions and other navigation tools guides us through the system." A "customized browser" is potentially the perfect tool for selecting, editing, packaging, manipulating, and controlling students' information.

We next learn that "ZapMe! editors search the Internet to collect ⁵³ and index information specifically focused for K-12 schools" (ZapMe! Web site n.d.). ZapMe! also tells us that they will be responsible for indexing and correlating this material to "a unified (National) curricular scope and sequence." They inform readers that they have "developed a proprietary-indexing scheme, which formats the content specifically for the K-12 market." Sorry, but who is supposed to choose and craft which information is best for students? ZapMe's executives? Not even close. And when they say they're going to "format" the content, I take it to mean they will cut it, slant it, shave it, dice it, tilt it, slice it, and wrap it all in glitzy technoid color, animation, video, and graphics—and ads. Too, "customized browsers" can short-circuit students' own discovery and thinking processes by directing them toward the ideas they are allowed to access—all the while leading them down endless electronic pathways strewn with ads. Finally, this ZapMe! quote refers to the "K-12 market." That's right; they define students as a "market." However, kids in schools were never, ever intended to be a "market." They are human beings who are required by law to be in school, which is supposed to be a marketplace of ideas, not a marketplace of Snickers, M&Ms, and Skittles. Students are learners, not merchandise to be hawked to advertisers in units-per-thousand.

ZapMe!'s Web site refers to its hardware and software as a "branded private electronic neighborhood." However, Mr. Rogers doesn't live there. Most residents in this neck of the woods will be surrounded by brands, if they are not walking brands themselves. Brands on every street corner, brands on every lawn, brands in every mailbox, brands lining every space down every winding boulevard to nowhere. These electronic messages will likely grow and change as marketers track the on-line movements of its young "visitors." Some current and new forms of Cyber-Salespeak (Robischon 1999) only suggest the possibilities. For instance, "interstitial ads" take shape on the screen, just slowly enough that, intrigued, you watch them materialize to see what they are. This, in essence, is a mini-commercial, which has a beginning, middle, and end. Watching this ad unfold allows you to participate in the message. This ad will disappear if you click to another page (where another one might be materializing).

"Pop-out ads" that appear in a smaller window next to the original Web page may be clicked on for an entire new venture into an infinite series of additional ads, some with video and audio features. "Banner ads" and "extramercials" wrap around the top of a screen and can even trail down the right-hand side, covering up the site's noncommercial content or information. Here again, *the act of moving this commercial* so you can read the actual content forces you to interact with the ad message and hence recall it better. Traditionally, a text's "editorial turf" or "message area" was sacred. Not anymore. It's like slapping a peel-off ad for Krazy Kola across a newspaper article reporting an airplane crash.

Another Cyber-Salespeak strategy is what I call "background tricks." For example, to focus attention on a new line of color printers, one Web site, known for its neon colors, turned its home page black and white. Increasingly, backgrounds (and many elements of foregrounds) will be composed of Salespeak. Finally, "animated ads" really capture attention. Most recently, to promote the Intel Corporation, the Web site for *USA Today* included an animated Homer Simpson scampering out of an advertisement and across the *USA Today* nameplate.

The leader in finding new ways to saturate the Web with 57 Salespeak is Procter & Gamble. The firm's vice president, Denis Beausejour, stated that his company has "a vested interest in making the Web the most effective marketing medium in history" (Greenstein 1999). Beausejour would like to see "bigger, more complicated ads that appear automatically in a separate window on the screen when you go to a website or that allow you to send e-mail from within the ad" (Greenstein 1999, 105). Sending e-mail from within an ad means that we'll be more internally active within the ad, which deepens Salespeak's effects on consumer attitudes and behaviors. Beausejour is also "experimenting with technology that automatically downloads an ad in the background" (Greenstein 1999, 105).

Salespeak will likely take up more and more space on television, 58 film, and computer screens, for more and more time, until they become a kind of wallpaper or permanent background. We will come to accept Salespeak as normal background, in addition to its increasing roles within various foregrounds (e.g., product placement ads). Especially in media, background serves as our anchor or base-point for "what is normal." When background and foreground are similar, they merge, just as for earlier generations, John Wayne, as actor and film character, became much the same as the open western landscape that so often spread out behind him. When Salespeak comes to dominate both background and foreground, our abilities to distinguish between the two will shrink and then disappear. . . .

NOTES FROM THE WORLD OF SALESPEAK

More than anything else, dominant voices may be shaped by their 59 environment. Consider the following facts about the environment that generates Salespeak:

- *$150 billion:* Amount spent by American advertisers each year, a cost that is passed on to consumers in higher prices. Landay (1998) summarizes our relationship with advertisers: "We pay their ad bills, we provide their profits, and we pay for their total tax write-off on the ads they place."
- *12 billion and 3 million:* The number of display ads and broadcast ads that Americans are collectively exposed to each day (Landay 1998).
- *2:* The number of times that we pay for advertising. First, advertising costs are built into the product. We pay again in terms of the time, money, and attention spent when processing an ad message.

- *1,000:* The number of chocolate chips in each bag of Chips Ahoy! cookies. The cookie company sponsored a "contest" in which students tried to confirm this claim (Labi 1999, 44).
- *$11 billion:* The amount of money dedicated to market research throughout the world (*World Opinion* Web site, November 11, 1998).
- *"Gosh, I don't understand—there are so many brands":* This is what one marketing firm has its researchers say, after they go into stores and place themselves next to real shoppers, in an effort to elicit what consumers are thinking in an authentic context (from the May 30, 1997, issue of the *Wall Street Journal* [McLaren 1998]).
- *$66 billion:* The amount of money spent by kids and young adults (ages 4–19) in 1992 (Bowen 1995).
- *16 million:* Approximate number of American children who use the Internet (*Brill's Content*, December 1998, 140).
- *115.95:* The number of banner ads viewed per week by the average Web user (*World Opinion* Web site, November 11, 1998).
- *"Save water. It's precious":* Message on a Coca-Cola billboard in Zimbabwe, where, according to the August 25, 1997, issue of the *Wall Street Journal*, the soft drink has become the drink of choice (necessity?) because of a water shortage (McLaren 1998).
- *$204 billion:* The estimated amount of Web-based transactions in 2001, up from $10.4 billion in 1997 (Zona Research 1999 on the *World Opinion* Web site).
- *89:* Percentage of children's Web sites that collect users' personal information (*Brill's Content*, December 1998, 140).
- *23:* Percentage of children's Web sites that tell kids to ask their parents for permission before sending personal information. (*Brill's Content*, December 1998, 140).
- *$29 million:* Net income for Nielsen Media Research during the first six months of 1998. (*Brill's Content*, December 1998, 140).
- *$36 billion:* The amount of money spent by kids and young adults in 1992 (ages 4–19) that belonged to their parents (Bowen 1995).
- *$3.4 million:* The amount of money received by the Grapevine-Colleyville Texas School District for displaying a huge Dr. Pepper logo atop the school roof. This school is in the flight path of Dallas-Fort Worth International Airport (Perrin 1997).

- *$8 million:* The amount of money received by the Colorado Springs School District in Colorado from Coca-Cola for an exclusive ten-year service agreement (Perrin 1997).
- *"A tight, enduring connection to teens":* What Larry Jabbonsky, a spokesman at Pepsi headquarters, said his company seeks (Perrin 1997).
- *9,000:* The number of items stocked in grocery stores in the 1970s (Will 1997).
- *30,000:* The number of items now stocked in grocery stores (Will 1997).
- *99:* The percentage of teens surveyed (N = 534 in four cities) who correctly identified the croaking frogs from a Budweiser television commercial (Horovitz and Wells 1997, 1A).
- *93:* The percentage of teens who reported that they liked the Budweiser frogs "very much" or "somewhat" (Horovitz and Wells 1997, 1A).
- *95 and 94:* The percentages of teens who know the Marlboro man and Joe Camel (Wells 1997, 1A).
- *Great Britain's white cliffs of Dover:* The backdrop for a laser-projected Adidas ad (Liu 1999).
- *$200 million:* The amount of money Miller Beer spends on advertising each year.
- *Time Warner:* A corporate empire that controls news and information in America. (There are fewer than twelve.) Time Warner owns large book publishers, cable TV franchises, home video firms, CNN and other large cable channels, and magazines such as Time, Life, People, Sports Illustrated, Money, Fortune, and Entertainment Weekly (Solomon 1999b).
- *$650 billion:* Annual sales of approximately 1,000 telemarketing companies, which employ 4 million Americans (Shenk 1999, 59).
- *350,000:* The number of classrooms that view two minutes of television commercials every day on Channel One ("Selling to School Kids" 1995).
- *154:* The number of Coca-Cola cans that students must find on a book cover and then color in, to reveal a hidden message ("Selling to School Kids" 1995).
- *50:* The percentage of increase in advertising expenditures during the past fifteen years (Bowen 1995).
- *560:* The daily number of ads targeted at the average American in 1971 (Shenk 1999, 59).

- *3,000:* The daily number of ads targeted at the average American in *1991 (Shenk 1999, 59).*
- *Business Update:* An hourly segment broadcast on National Public Radio. Even though NPR is supposed to focus on "public broadcasting," it does not offer a Labor Update.
- *3.4 trillion:* The number of e-mail messages that crossed the Internet in the United States in 1998—a number expected to double by 2001 (McCafferty 1999).
- *80 percent:* The percentage of America's e-mail messages in 1998 that were mass-produced e-mailings, "most from corporations with something to sell" (McCafferty 1998).

It's hardly unusual for a free enterprise system to employ 60 Salespeak. Advertising is a necessary ingredient for informing consumers about the goods and services they need. This is true for much of America's history. A sign hung in a trading post at the beginning of the Oregon Trail, 150 years ago, stating, "Sugar, 2 cents per lb.," contains necessary information for specific readers who had definite goals. Today, though, America is quite different.

First, unlike even forty years ago, most of today's advertising 61 carries scant information about the product or service. Second, the more affluent America becomes, the fewer true "needs" we have. To make up for it, advertisers now focus not so much on what we truly need, but on what we may desire. Third, very few limits are placed upon advertising: we have little control over where it appears, who can see it (note how many of the previous items focus on young people), how often it appears, how messages are constructed, or how much money is budgeted for them (at the expense of, say, improving the product). The field of advertising itself is now a major industry. The Bureau of Labor Statistics reports that in 1995, more people died on the job in advertising than in car factories, electrical repair companies, and petroleum refining operations (*Advertising Age,* August 19, 1996). Because advertising has such free rein in America, it's become one of our most dominating voices, if not the most dominating voice.

You're Soaking In It

Jennifer L. Pozner

"Advertisers know what womanpower is," explains a self- 1
promotional pitch for the *Ladies' Home Journal*. The ad shows a stylish
woman wired to a mammoth computer that measures her whims
with graphs, light bulbs and ticker tape. The magazine insists that,
like the machine, it has its finger on the pulse of women's desires.
Perk and breathlessness permeate its claim to be able to harness the
many elements of "womanpower," including "sales power" ("She
spots a bright idea in her favorite magazine, and suddenly the whole
town's sold on it!"), "will power" ("Can you stick to a nine-day diet
for more than four hours at a stretch?") and, of course, "purchasing
power" ("Isn't it the power of her purse that's been putting fresh
smiles on the faces of America's businessmen?").

That was 1958. Today advertisers are generally more sophisti- 2
cated in their execution, but their primary message to and about
women has remained fundamentally unchanged. To tap into our
power, offer us a new shade of lipstick, a fresh-scented floor wax or,
in the case of Mel Gibson's patronizing chick flick, *What Women
Want*, L'eggs pantyhose, Wonderbras or Nike Women's Sports gear.

The movie—No. 2 at the box office after a month in theaters— 3
stars Gibson as Nick Marshall, a pompous advertising executive
dubbed the "T&A King" for his successful reign over Swedish bikini-
babe commercials. But Nick's campaigns leave female consumers
cold and he loses an expected promotion to women's market whiz
Darcy Maguire (Helen Hunt). Nick's boss explains that while he's
more comfortable with Nick, men no longer dominate how ad dollars are being spent.

Once Nick acquires the ability to read women's minds—after an 4
unfortunate incident with volumizing mousse, a hair dryer and a
bathtub—a story unfolds that could only seem romantic to avid
Advertising Age readers: Nick and his nemesis Darcy fall in love over
Nike storyboards, brainstorming ways to convince consumers that
"Nike wants to empower women" and "Nike is state-of-the-art,
hardcore womanpower."

What Women Want is more than a commercial for Mars vs. Venus 5
gender typing; it's a feature-length product placement, a jarring
reminder that the entertainment media is up for grabs by the hawk-
ers of hair spray and Hondas. Which is not to say that the news

media is off limits. Take Disney's news giant, ABC. In November, after ABC accepted a hefty fee from Campbell's soup, journalist Barbara Walters and "The View" crew turned eight episodes of their talk show into paid infomercials for canned soup. Hosting a "soup-sipping contest" and singing the "M'm! M'm! Good!" jingle on-air, they made good on ABC's promise that the "hosts would try to weave a soup message into their regular on-air banter."

And in March, after Disney bought a stake in Pets.com, the com- 6 pany's snarky sock puppet mascot began appearing as a "guest" on "Good Morning America" and "Nightline." It was a sad day in news when Diane Sawyer addressed her questions to a sock on a stool with a guy's hand up its butt, but that's what passes for "synergy" in today's megamerged media climate.

How does advertising's increasing encroachment into every 7 niche of mass media impact our culture in general, and women in particular? Mothers Who Think asked pioneering advertising critic Jean Kilbourne, author of *Can't Buy My Love: How Advertising Changes the Way We Think and Feel*.

A favorite on the college lecture circuit, Kilbourne has produced 8 videos that are used as part of media literacy programs worldwide, in particular *Killing Us Softly*, first produced in 1979 and remade as *Killing Us Softly III* in 2000. She shares her thoughts here about advertising's effects on women, children, media and our cultural environment—and explains why salvation can't be found in a Nike sports bra.

In What Women Want, *Mel Gibson and Helen Hunt produce a Nike com-* 9 *mercial in which a woman runs in swooshed-up sportswear while a voice-over assures her that the road doesn't care if she's wearing makeup, and she doesn't have to feel uncomfortable if she makes more money than the road— basically equating freedom and liberation with a pair of $150 running shoes. Is this typical of advertising to women?*

Absolutely. The commercial in the movie is saying that women who 10 are unhappy with the quality of their relationships can ease their frustration by literally forming a more satisfying relationship with the road. There's no hint that her human relationships are going to improve, but the road will love her anyway.

Advertising is always about moving away from anything that 11 would help us find real change in our lives. In the funniest scene in the movie, when Mel Gibson finds out how much it hurts to wax his legs, he wonders, "Why would anyone do this more than once?"

That's a very good question. But, of course, the film doesn't go there. The real solutions—to stop waxing or to challenge unnatural beauty standards or to demand that men grow up—are never offered. Instead, the message is that we must continue with these painful and humiliating rituals, but at least we can escape for a while by lacing on our expensive sneakers and going out for a run.

What Women Want presents a pretty mercenary picture of advertising 12 *aimed at women. You've studied the industry for decades. Does it seem accurate to you?*

It isn't far off. As in the film, advertisers were kind of slow to really 13 focus on women. Initially they did it by co-opting feminism. Virginia Slims equated women's liberation and enslavement to tobacco with the trivializing slogan "You've come a long way, baby" in the '80s; a little while ago it ran a campaign with the slogan "Find your voice."

Then there were endless ads that turned the women's movement 14 into the quest for a woman's product. Was there ever such a thing as static cling before there were fabric softeners and sprays? More recently advertisers have discovered what they call "relationship marketing," creating ads that exploit a human need for connection and relationships, which in our culture is often seen as a woman's need.

Advertising and the larger culture often imply that women are failures if we 15 *do not have perfect relationships. Of course, "perfect" relationships don't exist in real life. Why are they so prominent in ads?*

This is part of the advertising mentality. Think about *What Women* 16 *Want*—there's an ad at the heart of this film literally and figuratively. Everybody lives in spectacular apartments, they're all thin and beautiful, and Mel Gibson makes this incredible instant transformation. He starts out as a jerk, he's callous, he tells degrading jokes and patronizes the women he works with, but because of his new mind-reading power he gains immediate insight into women. He becomes a great lover in the space of half an hour. At one point his daughter tells him he's never had a real relationship in his life, but by the end of the film he has authentic relationships with his daughter and his new love.

The truth is, most men gain insight into women not through 17 quick fixes but by having close relationships with them over time, sometimes painfully. In the world of advertising, relationships are instant and the best ones aren't necessarily with people: Zest is a soap, Happy is a perfume, New Freedom is a maxipad, Wonder is a bread, Good Sense is a tea bag and Serenity is a diaper. Advertising actually encourages us to have relationships with our products.

I'm looking at *TV Guide* right now and there's a Winston ciga-   18
rette ad on the back cover with a woman saying, "Until I find a real man, I'll take a real smoke." There's another with four different pictures of one man with four different women, and the copy reads, "Who says guys are afraid of commitment? He's had the same backpack for years." In another ad, featuring a young woman wearing a pretty sweater, the copy says, "The ski instructor faded away after one session. Fortunately the sweater didn't."

One automobile spot implied that a Civic coupe would never tell   19
you, "It's not you, it's me. I need more space. I'm not ready for a commitment." Maybe our chances for lasting relationships are greater with our cars than with our partners, but surely the solution can't be to fall in love with our cars, or to depend on them rather than on each other.

Basically, men can't be trusted but Häagen-Dazs never disappoints? Love is   20
fleeting but a diamond is forever? Sort of a recipe for lowered expectations,
isn't it?

A central message of advertising is that relationships with human   21
beings can't be counted on, especially for women. The message is that men will make commitments only reluctantly and can't be trusted to keep them. Straight women, and these are pretty much the women in ads, are told that it's normal not to expect very much or get very much from the men in their lives. This normalizes really abnormal behavior—with male violence at the extreme and male callousness in general—by reinforcing men's unwillingness to express their feelings. This harms men, of course, as well as women.

In What Women Want, *Mel Gibson is literally able to "get into the female*   22
psyche," private thoughts and all, after he waxes his hairy legs and
crams them into a pair of L'eggs pantyhose. Is it unusual for advertisers
to imply that the essence of womanhood can be found in cosmetics and
commercialism?

Not at all. The central message of advertising has to be that we are   23
what we buy. And perhaps what's most insidious about this is that it takes very human, very real feelings and desires such as the need to

love and be loved, the need for authentic connection, the need for meaningful work, for respect, and it yokes these feeling to products. It tells us that our ability to attain love depends upon our attractiveness.

By now most of us know that these images are unrealistic and unhealthy, 24 *that implants leak, anorexia and bulimia can kill and, in real life, model Heidi Klum has pores. So why do the images in ads still have such away over us?*

Most people like to think advertising doesn't affect them. But if that 25 were really true, why would companies spend over $200 billion a year on advertising? Women don't buy into this because we're shallow or vain or stupid but because the stakes are high. Overweight women do tend to face biases—they're less likely to get jobs; they're poorer. Men do leave their wives for younger, more beautiful women as their wives age. There is manifest contempt and real-life consequences for women who don't measure up. These images work to keep us in line.

What do these images teach girls about what they can expect from them- 26 *selves, from boys, from sex, from each other?*

Girls get terrible messages about sex from advertising and popular 27 culture. An ad featuring a very young woman in tight jeans reads: "He says the first thing he noticed about you is your great personality. He lies." Girls are told that boys are out for sex at all times, and girls should always look as if they are ready to give it. (But God help them if they do.) The emphasis for girls and women is always on being desirable, not being agents of their own desire. Girls are supposed to somehow be innocent and seductive, virginal and experienced, all at the same time.

Girls are particularly targeted by the diet industry. The obsession 28 with thinness is about cutting girls down to size, making sure they're not too powerful in any sense of the word. One fashion ad I use in my presentations shows an extremely thin, very young Asian woman next to the copy "The more you subtract, the more you add."

Adolescent girls constantly get the message that they should 29 diminish themselves, they should be less than what they are. Girls are told not to speak up too much, not to be too loud, not to have a hearty appetite for food or sex or anything else. Girls are literally shown being silenced in ads, often with their hands over their mouth or, as in one ad, with a turtleneck sweater pulled up over their mouth.

One ad sold lipstick with a drawing of a woman's lips sucking 30
on a pacifier. A girl in a particularly violent entertainment ad has her
lips sewn shut. Sometimes girls are told to keep quiet in other ways,
by slogans like "Let your fingers do the talking" (an ad for nail pol-
ish), "Watch your mouth, young lady" (for lipstick), "Make a state-
ment without saying a word" (for perfume), "Score high on
non-verbal skills" (for a clothing store).

Let's talk about violence against women in ads. A controversy broke out dur- 31
ing the Olympics when NBC ran a Nike commercial parodying slasher
films, in which Olympic runner Suzy Favor Hamilton is chased by a villain
with a chain saw. Hamilton outruns him, leaving the would-be murderer
wheezing in the woods. The punch line? "Why sport? You'll live longer."
The ad shocked many people, but isn't violence against women, real or
implied, common in ads?

People were outraged that Nike considered this type of thing a joke. 32
A recent Perry Ellis sequence showed a woman apparently dead in a
shower with a man standing over her; that one drew protests, too.
But ads often feature images of women being threatened, attacked, or
killed. Sexual assault and battery are normalized, even eroticized.

In one ad a woman lies dead on a bed with her breasts exposed 33
and her hair sprawled out around her, and the copy reads, "Great
hair never dies." A perfume ad that ran in several teen magazines
showed a very young woman with her eyes blackened, next to the
text "Apply generously to your neck so he can smell the scent as you
shake your head 'no.'" In other words, he'll understand that you
don't really mean it when you say no, and he can respond like any
other animal.

An ad for a bar in Georgetown with a close-up of a cocktail had 34
the headline "If your date won't listen to reason, try a velvet ham-
mer." That's really dangerous when you consider how many sexual
assaults involve alcohol in some way. We believe we are not affected
by these images, but most of us experience visceral shock when we
pay conscious attention to them.

Are there subtler forms of abuse in ads? 35

There's a lot of emotional violence in ads. For example, in one 36
cologne ad a handsome man ignores two beautiful blonds. The copy
reads, "Do you want to be the one she tells her deep, dark secrets to?
Or do you want to be her deep, dark secret?" followed by a final

instruction: "Don't be such a good boy." What's the deep, dark secret here? That he's sleeping with both of them? On one level the message is that the way to get beautiful women is to ignore them, perhaps mistreat them. The message to men is that emotional intimacy is not a good thing. This does terrible things to men, and of course to women too.

There are also many, many ads in which women are pitted against 37 each other for male attention. For example, there's one ad with a top-less woman on a bed and the copy "What the bitch who's about to steal your man wears." Other ads feature young women fighting or glaring at each other. This means that when girls hit adolescence, at a time when they most need support from each other, they're encouraged to turn on each other in competition for men. It's tragic, because the truth is that one of the most powerful antidotes to destructive cultural messages is close and supportive female friendships.

Over the years we've grown more accustomed to product placements in 38 *movies, but* What Women Want *takes advertiser-driven content to a new level. I tried to keep a running count, but there were so many I lost track: Sears, L'eggs, Wonderbra, Macintosh, Martha Stewart, CNN, Meredith Brooks and Alanis Morissette CD covers all get prominent plugs.*

The final commercial Gibson pitches to the Nike reps was similar in 39 *style, tone and prime-time-friendly slogan to sports ads we've seen on TV before. Would you be surprised if Nike's fake ad eventually traveled from the big screen to the small screen? How did we get to a point where the whole premise of a film rests on product placements?*

I wouldn't be surprised at all. In fact, the ad in the movie was made 40 in connection with Wieden + Kennedy, Nike's real-life ad agency. But Nike doesn't really need to pay to broadcast the commercial on TV, since this film was so successful at the box office—there couldn't be a better launch for a commercial than this movie.

I think this is the wave of the future. As more and more people 41 use their VCR to skip the commercials when they watch television, the commercials will begin to become part of the program so they can't be edited out. So while you're watching "Friends," Jennifer Aniston will say to Courteney Cox, "Your hair looks great," and Courteney will say, "Yeah, I'm using this new gel!"

A number of media critics have dubbed the encroachment of advertising 42 *in media, education and public spaces "ad creep." You've called it a "toxic cultural environment." Can you explain that?*

As the mother of a 13-year-old girl, I feel I'm raising my daughter in   43
a toxic cultural environment. I hate that advertisers cynically equate
rebellion with smoking, drinking and impulsive and impersonal sex.
I want my daughter to be a rebel, to defy stereotypes of "femininity,"
but I don't want her to put herself in danger. I feel I have to fight the
culture every step of the way in terms of messages she gets.

Just as it is difficult to raise kids safely in a physically toxic envi-   44
ronment, where they're breathing polluted air or drinking toxic
water, it's also difficult or even impossible to raise children in a culturally toxic environment, where they're surrounded by unhealthy
images about sex and relationships, and where their health is constantly sacrificed for the sake of profit.

Even our schools are toxic—when McDonald's has a nutrition   45
curriculum, Exxon has an environmental curriculum and kindergart-
ners are given a program called "Learning to read through recogniz-
ing corporate logos." Education is tainted when a student can get
suspended for wearing a Pepsi T-shirt on a school-sponsored Coke
day, which happened in Georgia in 1998.

The United States is one of the few nations in the world that   46
think that children are legitimate targets for advertisers. We allow the
tobacco and alcohol industries to use talking frogs and lizards to sell
beer and cartoon characters to sell cigarettes. The Budweiser commercials are in fact the most popular commercials with elementary
school kids, and Joe Camel is now as recognizable to 6-year-olds as is
Mickey Mouse.

What advice do you have for parents, for any of us, who want to counteract   47
this toxic cultural environment?

Parents can talk to their children, make these messages conscious. We   48
can educate ourselves and become media literate. But primarily we
need to realize that this is not something we can fight purely on an
individual basis.

Corporations are forever telling us that if we don't like what's on   49
TV we should just turn it off, not let our kids watch tobacco ads or
violent movies. We constantly hear that if parents would just talk to
their kids there would be no problem. But that really is like saying,
"If your children are breathing poisoned air, don't let them breathe."

We need to join together to change the toxic cultural environ-   50
ment. That includes things such as lobbying to teach noncorporate
media literacy in our schools, fighting to abolish or restrict advertising aimed at children, organizing to get ads out of our schools, ban-

ning the promotion of alcohol and tobacco, and other community solutions.

There are great media literacy projects in Los Angeles, New 51 Mexico, Massachusetts and many places throughout the world. There's no quick fix, but I have extensive resources about media criticism groups, social change organizations, educational material, media literacy programs and more available on my Web site. If they want, people could start there.

ACKNOWLEDGMENTS